The Real Estate Agent's Ultimate Tax Saving Guide

The Best Tax Tips and Techniques for
Real Estate Professionals

New and updated for 2020!

Copyright 2020 by Brad Hennebert

This material may not be reproduced, stored in a retrieval system, or transmitted in whole or in part, in any form or by any means without the written permission of the publisher and the copyright holder. Author's forms and worksheets in the book may be reproduced for the personal use of the purchaser, and may not be republished in any manner without express written permission. IRS Forms are for public use. Photo images used are under license from Shutterstock.com, unless author's credit is under that specific image.

The publisher nor author rendering tax, legal, accounting, or other professional advice and assume no liability. Users of this book must see their personal advisors to ensure proper implementation and individual applicability of the ideas presented in herein.

Do you have these Challenges or Struggles?

- Angry or fearful that you may be leaving money on the table by missing tax deductions you don't know about?

- Feel like you work 60+ hours a week and don't have enough to show for it?

- You don't have enough money left over to pay bills or buy the things your family needs, even though you are making a lot of money?

- You owe the IRS money, and think you cannot afford to pay?

- Afraid to spend money because you're not sure how much you're going to owe on taxes next year?

- Put off home improvements and vacations because your income from real estate is so unpredictable?

- Do you make good money, but still have debt you cannot dig out of?

- Do you avoid some legitimate tax deductions because you're afraid of being audited?

- Do you have that nagging feeling that the 'Tax Software in a Box' or the temp employee at the national tax preparation chain doesn't really have the in-depth knowledge to give you sophisticated finance and tax advice needed of Real Estate pros?

- Do you face either high self-employment tax or alternative minimum tax?

- Have years of unfiled tax returns, and terrified the IRS is going to catch up to you soon?

- Don't know what to do, and would be embarrassed if others knew?

We have the answers!

TABLE OF CONTENTS

INTRODUCTION 3
HOW TO USE THIS BOOK 6
MONEY SAVING QUICK-START TIPS 8

THE BEST TAX TACTICS FOR REAL ESTATE AGENTS
    SET UP AN S CORP 9
    MAKE YOUR PERSONAL CAR YOUR BUSINESS CAR 15
    THE WONDERFUL HOME OFFICE DEDUCTION 17
    SECTION 105 HEALTH REIMBURSEMENT PLAN 26
    PAY YOUR KIDS 31

MAXIMIZING DEDUCTIONS
    SEPARATE BUSINESS VS. PERSONAL EXPENSES 33
    RECORDS YOU MUST KEEP TO CLAIM DEDUCTIONS 37
    BUSINESS EXPENSES 39
    VEHICLE EXPENSES 41
    IRS MILEAGE / AUTO EXPENSE AUDITS 42
    METHODS FOR MAXIMIZING YOUR MILEAGE DEDUCTIONS 48
    MILEAGE VS. ACTUAL EXPENSE 49
    MEALS AND ENTERTAINMENT 50
    BUSINESS MEALS 51
    HEALTH INSURANCE FOR THE SELF-EMPLOYED 56
    QUALIFIED SMALL BUSINESS HEALTH REIMBURSEMENT ARRANGEMENT 56
    CASHING IN ON THE TAX CUTS AND JOBS ACT CHANGES 58
    CHOICE OF BUSINESS ENTITY 60
    GENERAL S CORP FORMATION QUALIFICATIONS 63
    1120S FORM K1 64
    S CORP DRAWBACKS 66
    RETROACTIVE S CORP ELECTION 67
    C CORPORATIONS MAKE A COMEBACK 69

STAY OUT OF TROUBLE WITH THE IRS
    COMMON TAX MYTHS THAT CAN GET YOU INTO TROUBLE 70
    PRESENTATIONS VS. BUSINESS MEALS 52
    ESTIMATED TAXES 53

IRS PAYMENT PLANS AND IRS PROBLEM RESOLUTION
    UNFILED TAX RETURNS 75
    SUBSTITUTE FOR RETURN (SFR) 78
    DON'T PUT A BULLSEYE ON YOUR BACK 83
    IRS TAX DEBT RESOLUTION 85
    INSTALLMENT AGREEMENTS 86

OFFER IN COMPROMISE 93
IRS COLLECTIONS 96
REASONABLE COLLECTION POTENTIAL.. 96
ALLOWABLE LIVING EXPENSES 100
THE COLLECTION STATUTE EXPIRATION DATE (CSED)................... 102
IRS LIENS 104
LIEN SUBORDINATION.. 105
IRS LEVIES 107
GARNISHMENTS / WAGE LEVIES 108

TAXES AND YOUR CLIENTS
PRIMARY RESIDENCE CAPITAL GAINS TAX EXCLUSION................... 109
1031 LIKE-KIND EXCHANGES 113
SECTION 1033 INVOLUNTARY CONVERSIONS 118
RENTAL INCOME AND EXPENSES 119
RENTALS AS A BUSINESS 125
SECTION 1231 125
HOME OFFICE EXPENSES FOR RENTAL PROPERTIES 126
MEETINGS, SEMINARS, AND CONVENTIONS....................................... 127
SECTION 179 EXPENSING 127
SALE OF RENTAL PROPERTIES 128
INSTALLMENT SALES 131
REAL ESTATE AGENT S CORP ISSUES IN OHIO................................... 131
LOCAL TAXES FOR OHIO REAL ESTATE AGENTS 133
GET STARTED NOW 136

INTRODUCTION

I wrote this book because I have seen taxpayers break every rule and disregard every piece of advice it contains. I've met clients who overpaid their taxes by tens of thousands of dollars needlessly. I've also had armed IRS and FBI agents come to my office with subpoenas seeking information regarding former clients who *did not* heed my advice.

The monetary costs of these blunders and the incalculable anxiety the associated IRS problems created, were totally avoidable. By adhering to straightforward best practices and uncomplicated tax strategies, real estate agents (and any other self-employed individuals) can set themselves and their businesses up to maximize the amount of money they actually keep, and minimize any tax worries they have.

In the course of preparing thousands of tax returns for real estate agents, and working with them intimately, I realized early on that most were in desperate need of more advanced tax advisory services. By advisory services, I mean real estate agents needed professionally developed tax strategies and tactics, and a business tax plan to approach to each year. Most agents would actually be well served to have consultations during the year too.

Haphazard tax prep with planning costs many agents the fruits of 1-2 closings in extra tax money paid *each year*. You know how hard you work for each deal, why give away the proceeds of 1 or 2 of those?

Real estate professionals are not well served by the fast-food kind of tax service where you show up with a folder of documents and sit at a desk across from the tax guy for an hour while he goes through the questions that pop up on his computer screen. Then he prints it out and you see them again next year, with no advice, no follow up and no intensive guidance during the year.

Real estate agents are far better served by a trusted advisor, a specialist if you will, who deals regularly with the complexities and nuances of the real estate business. Many tax preparers have one or two real estate agent clients, and don't know the difference between a commission split and a desk fee, but still profess to be experts.

They honestly don't know much about how the real estate business works and can inadvertently get agents into a lot of trouble. Most commonly, they cause their clients to pay far more in taxes than they should. We endeavor to save you every nickel we possibly can, legally and appropriately. If that means changing your business structure and tracking your expenses far more diligently, that's what we'll recommend.

Agents are ambitious, highly-motived professionals, and they work very hard expending tremendous amounts of energy putting together deals – the product of which is the money they earn. I find nothing more professionally disappointing than seeing an agent work hard all year, and then end up paying sometimes double the tax they would have, wasting half their profit sometimes, out of sheer ignorance of tax strategy. I look at it as foolishly squandering hundreds of hours of your time. For no other reason than a lack of knowledge, probably coupled with inadequate professional advice.

I frequently meet agents making $100,000 or more who have

overpaid their taxes by $10,000 or more. They were initially delighted to tell us they only paid their tax guy $200, or they did their own taxes online and "saved" money, believing all tax advisors and tax advice to be the same.

Why work that hard all year, only to needlessly and stupidly give the government the fruits of nearly half your net profit? When we unpack this for new clients and diagram it out with real numbers -- well, let's just say there is a reason we always have a box of Kleenex in our conference rooms. What you don't know can and will hurt you, especially regarding your money and your taxes.

One agent I'd known for almost a decade finally became a client after her accountant retired. I changed up some things for her and saved her over $20,000 more than what her other guy was doing – the first year. That's $20,000 in tax savings the first year. Over the ten years of returns I examined, my strategies would have saved her over $200,000. But that money was lost forever - needlessly donated to the government through ignorance and trusting a tax advisors who really didn't understand real estate professionals.

The Kleenex got used that day, believe me.

I am not going to help you earn more. I will significantly and meaningfully increase the amount money you keep.

May the reader take advantage of whatever wisdom is presented, and know that much of it came from the exposure to the costly financial mistakes of others. It is offered so that you don't have to learn these lessons the hard way.

HOW TO USE THIS BOOK

The volume is written with the most important information right up front. The items that will save the most real estate agents the most money are at the very beginning, with illustrative anecdotes and practical suggestions. The biggest impact tax strategies are in the first section – The Best Tax Tactics for Real Estate Agents.

As the book progresses, it delves more deeply into many more detailed and specific tax and financial approaches that may save one agent thousands of dollars per year, and yet not be applicable at all to another agent. You will quickly see that the varying individual lifestyle, family and business circumstances of each taxpayer determine if a tax strategy may work for them at all.

The second section is about maximizing tax deductions, most of which can be boiled down to properly documenting and segregating business expenses, the purpose of which is to lower your taxable income. Every dollar of legitimate expense we can document will lower your taxes, and many agents will find this section very useful in clarifying their thinking and structuring their business finances to maximize their financial efficiency.

For your convenience, every general topic is listed out in the table of contents, and feel free to skim the deductions section for items that interest you. As we've found somewhere around 1-in-8 real estate agents has some IRS tax issue, the section IRS Payment Plans and IRS Problem Resolution has some very detailed references and methods to set up IRS payment plans and resolve IRS issues.
I invite you to read the book through and soak it all in, or skim

it and get a flavor for what you'd like to do, and then zero in on that.

The appendix contains many of the worksheets and forms we commonly use in our practice and give to our clients.

The strategies and methods in this system are geared toward normally motived real estate professionals and it takes little in the way of financial investment to make them succeed. No special skills or especially challenging work are required. You will have to apply what you learn, however! The financial magic doesn't just happen by itself.

I'm confident that you'll find the strategies, tactics and techniques here will generate *100 times* the dollar amount you paid for the book just in the form of tax savings. Just one (legal) tax technique we advocate many real estate agents use saves our average client that uses it $*8,000 -$17,000 per year in taxes.*

This is not a "How to do a 1040" course, that's not the goal at all. Use this manual as a high-level strategic tool and to help you formulate a plan tailored to you and your tax situation. You'll probably still want to use a qualified tax practitioner to prepare your tax return. Think of it this way: The goal here is to dramatically increase the amount of money you keep by the end of the tax year, not to teach you the boring and complex minutia of doing a tax return yourself.

Brad Hennebert
Founder, Realty Income Tax Advisors

Money Saving Quick Start Tips

Action Item		BENEFIT
Consider setting your real estate business up as an S Corporation	✔	Average Real Estate Agent Saves $8,000 - $17,000
Open a Business Bank Account (and use it for only business)	✔	Provides necessary expense documentation and maximize your tax deductions. Necessary to separate business from personal
Get a Business Credit Card (if you use credit cards at all)	✔	Builds necessary expense documentation and maximize your tax deductions
Track all your mileage/vehicle expenses (get an ap!)	✔	Builds necessary expense documentation, and maximize your tax deductions
Maximize your Home Office Deduction	✔	Don't leave $3,500 + on the table!
Pay your Estimated Taxes or payroll withholding	✔	Avoid nasty surprise on April 15th, comply with tax law
Establish a Section 105 Medical Reimbursement Plan	✔	Average client saves $3,000 annually
Pay your kids or spouse	✔	A great way to claim a deduction for what you may already be doing
Elect to make your personal car your 'business' car	✔	For 2019 you can deduct the fair market value of the car at the business use percentage!

SECTION 1: THE BEST TAX TACTICS FOR REAL ESTATE AGENTS

#1 BEST TAX TIP: SET UP AN S CORP

And it is this last way of an LLC electing to be taxed as an S Corporation structure that probably offers the most tax advantages for high-earning real estate professionals. The benefits include corporate financial liability protection, and yet the biggest advantage is in the reduction of payroll taxes.

PULL OUT YOUR TAX RETURN FROM LAST YEAR AND LOOK AT LINE 57, ON PAGE 2. It's on Schedule 4 (Form 1040), line 57 on your 1040. This is your self-employment tax. Many of our new real estate agent clients had paid <u>over $15,000 every year</u> on this, prior to coming to us!

Filing your taxes as an S Corporation allows you to have all the same liability advantages as any other LLC structure, but it allows for pass-through treatment for Federal tax purposes. All the corporation's income, expenses, tax credits, etc., pass-through from the company to the owner.

For example, a real estate agent client of ours had a net profit on her real estate activities on her Schedule C of $135,000. Her income tax was $25,199. But her self-employment tax was an additional $19,075, for a total tax bill of $44,274 That's a huge chunk of money to pay on an income of $135,000! Self-employment taxes are your share of Social

Security and Medicare taxes that you pay. For instance, the wage limit for 2020 for maximum social security withholding is $137,700, meaning the most you'd pay for the Social Security portion of self-employment tax for the 2019 tax year is 12.4% of $137,700 or $17,0748. There is another 2.9% on top of that goes toward Medicare, and there is no cut-off limit to that. You deduct a portion of the self-employment tax on your 1040.

The real beauty of an S Corporation is that there is the reduction of payroll taxes for the owners that is not available otherwise. To take advantage of this, a business owner must elect to be taxed as an S Corp by filing a form 2553 with the IRS. I recommend you have a competent business accountant do it, as I've *never seen a taxpayer do a 2553 correctly* on their own, and a mistake made here could be very costly and irreversible.

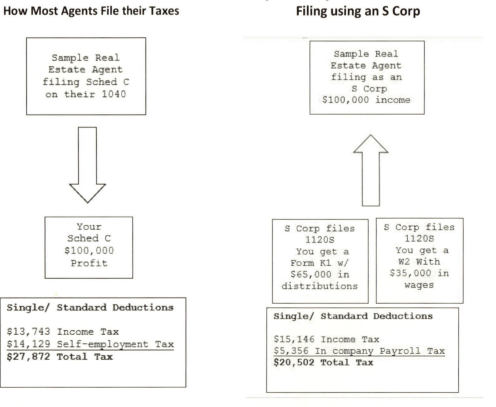

Let's say, for example, you are a real estate agent who had a net $100,000 income, just from your real estate activity. For our example below, let's say for the Schedule C you had $100,000 in profits. For the S-Corp example, everything is the same, except you paid yourself a salary of $35,000 on a W2, and took $65,000 as distributions.

Business Structure		Total
Schedule C:	Your total Tax Would be:	$27,872
S-Corporation:	Your total payroll tax would be: (both your half + the company's half)	$20,502
	As an S Corp you save:	**$7,370**

Yes, that's right, you save a whopping $7,370 in total tax on a $100,000 income. You're asking, what's the catch? Paperwork -- payroll tax filing paperwork.

To take full advantage of the S Corp status as an owner of an S Corp, you must pay yourself a reasonable salary, and that salary is subject to normal taxes on a W2 like any other employee. However, the profits you receive on top that you could take as distributions. Those distributions are not subject to self-employment tax, and that's what you save. Of course, the more you make, the more you can save.

Note that your <u>total income</u> is going to be the same if you are a Schedule C as with an S Corporation, but tax allocation of it is different. In both cases you made $100,000. With the S Corp structure, you just save a lot of money!

Now we are going to get deep in the weeds on the mechanics of it, but right before we do: <u>You can pay a small price to go to a local tax expert to set this up.</u> Most accountants will do it for

$500-$1,000, and most tax attorneys charge a bit more. Tell them (or call us, for that matter): "I want to be an S-Corp and save thousands of dollars, help me set it up." And they should be able to get that done and guide you through all the minutia.

You can even elect to be an S Corp retroactively, if you have an LLC or corporation already set up, under IRS Revenue Procedure 2013-30!

We will take an LLC you set up or already have, and we will file the 2553 with the IRS and get you set up as an S Corp.

But jumping through all those hoops is absolutely necessary to be able to save you the reduction in the payroll taxes. Again, you can just have a tax pro set it up for you without much expense, now that you know the "secret"!

Back to the *minutia*: You do have to pay yourself a reasonable salary, so the IRS at least gets some payroll tax from you. There is a Tax Court case right on the subject of reasonable salary just for real estate agents, where the IRS determined the median hourly wage for real estate agents in a zip code, and multiplied it by 2080 work hours in a year.

According to studies we use to advise clients, we found the median salaried real estate agent income in for 2019 was a bit over $57,000 in our home state of Ohio. If you made less than $57,000 in commissions we'd adjust that salary number down.

There is a much more elaborate matrix of criteria the IRS can use if they want to examine your S Corp reasonable salary, and they will want to see what the owner-employee did for the S corporation to earn their compensation.

Like most all real estate agents, the money you bring in is based almost all on the results of your personal efforts. If and when an IRS auditor thinks all of the profits you make are just from the owners' personal services, then they may want to think that most of the profit distribution should be allocated as compensation with payroll taxes taken out. Having employees, contractors, or any other kind of paid helpers can assist you in having this argument with the IRS should you be stuck in an audit.

As a S Corp, your real estate business will report your income from that business in two ways: first on the W2 you'll get for your reasonable salary, and secondly the distributions you take that are not subject to self-employment tax will be reported on a Form K1 that will be part of your S Corp return, and the information from the K1 will flow through to your personal 1040. Note: you do get a ½ deduction on self-employment taxes that go on the front page of your 1040, and we have taken that into account in our examples.

This does have a cost, and for most owner-only S Corps it's $1,000 or so annually for a payroll company to do this for you and a small fraction of that for the software to file your own, or you can do your own payroll. That means you need to file not just your annual W2/W3, but the quarterly 941s which are forms the company would file reporting wages and withholdings, the 940 which is Federal unemployment taxes, and any state and city returns that are due. My advice is to hire a payroll company to do it for you, as professional payroll services are relatively inexpensive, while the cost of payroll tax mistakes can be quite high.

#2 BIGGEST TAX TIP: CONVERT YOUR VEHICLE TO BE YOUR 'BUSINESS' VEHICLE

It's a given that real estate agents spend a lot of time in their cars. Wouldn't it be nice if you could get a much bigger tax deduction from your car than just taking the amount you get for mileage or adding up your gas receipts every year?

The Tax Cuts and Jobs Act gives a nice tax break to business Entrepreneurs such as real estate agents this year. To make this happen, you need to take your personal vehicle and make it your business' vehicle. Your former personal vehicle will then be able to generate you a tax deduction of up to 100% of its fair market value.

If Sally has a 2019 Subaru worth $40,000 and transfers it to her realty business, and she uses it 80% for business; 20% personal, she can take a $32,000 tax deduction for 2020 ($40,000 x 80% personal use = $32,000) on a bonus depreciation qualifying vehicle. The percentage math works the same if you buy a new car this year, and it doesn't matter if you have a loan balance on the car or not.

When you take a personal vehicle and convert it to business use, under the eyes of the IRS they see you as placing the car 'into' the business at that time. That means you can start depreciating the car and claim the associated deduction.

To determine how to do that, you use the lesser of the amount of the fair market on the date of conversion from personal to business use or use the adjusted basis of the car. Generally, you look at the Kelly Blue Book or other sales price date to come up with the fair market value.

If you buy a new car, you take the price you pay for the car. For instance, your new car is $30,000, and you maybe use it 70% for business, your tax deduction is $30,000 x 70% = $21,000. The sales tax paid is deductible as a business expense at 70%, and the remaining 30% would be an itemized deduction on your Schedule A. This is a great reason to buy a new car in this year!

Keep in mind, you STILL get to deduct your operating costs, like gas, insurance, maintenance, repairs, car washes, etc.!

#3 BIGGEST TAX TIP: THE WONDERFUL HOME OFFICE DEDUCTION

My view on home office deductions: If you qualify for it – take it!

Home office expense is another item we see audited frequently with real estate agents, right after mileage. The IRS has figured out, through much experience, where people tend to cheat, and they target those items heavily on audits. But keep your records in order, and you'll have nothing to fear!

In today's fast-paced environment where offers come quick and responses are needed *right now*, it is almost unavoidable to work at home after hours, <u>almost every day</u>, in some manner. Even if you have an office available to you and pay desk fees, you probably still work at home.

Nobody said real estate was a 9 to 5 job!

For home office expenses, self-employed individuals can expense a portion of their home and related expenditures related to their workspace. The key is that workspace must be *regularly* and *exclusively* used for business. Some taxpayers hear the 'regularly,' and have visions of writing off their dining room table.

It's the 'exclusive' part where some lose their hearing, and that means that the workspace is used only for business. Nothing else. To put it succinctly: Your home office space must be used 100% for business, only.

That is where some taxpayers end up not truly qualifying for the home office deduction, because their husband uses the home office every day to check his Facebook and buy stuff on eBay, their daughter practices clarinet there, and a hundred other things. Sorry, I'm just reporting the rules as they are, not as I wish they were!

Here's a direct quote from IRS Publication 587 on what constitutes allowable home office expenses:

> *"To qualify to deduct expenses for business use of your home, you must use part of your home:*
> - *Exclusively and regularly as your principal place of business (see Principal Place of Business, later);*
> - *Exclusively and regularly as a place where you meet or deal with patients, clients, or customers in the normal course of your trade or business;*
> - *In the case of a separate structure which is not attached to your home, in connection with your trade or business;*
> - *On a regular basis for certain storage use (see Storage of inventory or product samples, later);*
> - *For rental use (see Pub. 527); or*
> - *As a daycare facility (see Daycare Facility, later)."*
> - **From IRS Publication 587, 2017**

I know what you're asking: How's the IRS going to know if someone else uses the office or it's not 100 % business? Believe me, I understand, I'm just telling you the rules. I end up working at home almost every night, and I still don't take a home office deduction because my 'home office' is usually my kitchen table with a laptop after my kids go to bed.

If you do use your home office regularly and exclusively for business, you can expense a portion of your house-related expenses. See the hypothetical example below:

Home office Square Footage	210
Total House Square Footage	2,500
Business % Use	8.40%

House Expenses:	Indirect Expense for Whole House	Expenses for Home Office
Mortgage interest & PMI	$ 7,500	$ 630
Real estate taxes	3,500	294
Or Rent (if you rent)		
Homeowners insurance	500	42
Utilities:		
Internet, home phone (@ 50% business use)	1,000	500
Electric	650	55
Gas	450	38
Water	150	13
Whole Structure Repairs and maintenance (roof, etc.)	2,250	189
Total	$15,000	$1,760
Total indirect & direct expenses	$16,760	
Business percentage of home for indirect expenses from above	8.40%	
Amount of Home Office Deduction	**$1,408**	

IRS Form 8829, on the next page, is what you use on your tax return to figure your home office deduction on your tax return.

Form 8829
Department of the Treasury
Internal Revenue Service (99)

Expenses for Business Use of Your Home
▶ File only with Schedule C (Form 1040 or 1040-SR). Use a separate Form 8829 for each home you used for business during the year.
▶ Go to www.irs.gov/Form8829 for instructions and the latest information.

OMB No. 1545-0074

2019

Attachment Sequence No. **176**

Name(s) of proprietor(s) | Your social security number

Part I — Part of Your Home Used for Business

1. Area used regularly and exclusively for business, regularly for daycare, or for storage of inventory or product samples (see instructions) **1**
2. Total area of home **2**
3. Divide line 1 by line 2. Enter the result as a percentage .... **3** %
   For daycare facilities not used exclusively for business, go to line 4. All others, go to line 7.
4. Multiply days used for daycare during year by hours used per day . . **4** hr.
5. If you started or stopped using your home for daycare during the year, see instructions; otherwise, enter 8,760 .... **5** hr.
6. Divide line 4 by line 5. Enter the result as a decimal amount . . . . **6** .
7. Business percentage. For daycare facilities not used exclusively for business, multiply line 6 by line 3 (enter the result as a percentage). All others, enter the amount from line 3 .... ▶ **7** %

Part II — Figure Your Allowable Deduction

8. Enter the amount from Schedule C, line 29, **plus** any gain derived from the business use of your home, **minus** any loss from the trade or business not derived from the business use of your home (see instructions) **8**

See instructions for columns (a) and (b) before completing lines 9–22.

	(a) Direct expenses	(b) Indirect expenses
9. Casualty losses (see instructions) **9**		
10. Deductible mortgage interest (see instructions) . **10**		
11. Real estate taxes (see instructions) **11**		
12. Add lines 9, 10, and 11 .... **12**		

13. Multiply line 12, column (b), by line 7 . . . . **13**
14. Add line 12, column (a), and line 13 .... **14**
15. Subtract line 14 from line 8. If zero or less, enter -0- **15**

16. Excess mortgage interest (see instructions) . . **16**		
17. Excess real estate taxes (see instructions) . . **17**		
18. Insurance **18**		
19. Rent **19**		
20. Repairs and maintenance **20**		
21. Utilities **21**		
22. Other expenses (see instructions) **22**		
23. Add lines 16 through 22 .... **23**		

24. Multiply line 23, column (b), by line 7 . . . . **24**
25. Carryover of prior year operating expenses (see instructions) **25**
26. Add line 23, column (a), line 24, and line 25 .... **26**
27. Allowable operating expenses. Enter the **smaller** of line 15 or line 26 .... **27**
28. Limit on excess casualty losses and depreciation. Subtract line 27 from line 15 .... **28**
29. Excess casualty losses (see instructions) **29**
30. Depreciation of your home from line 42 below **30**
31. Carryover of prior year excess casualty losses and depreciation (see instructions) **31**
32. Add lines 29 through 31 .... **32**
33. Allowable excess casualty losses and depreciation. Enter the **smaller** of line 28 or line 32 . . . **33**
34. Add lines 14, 27, and 33 .... **34**
35. Casualty loss portion, if any, from lines 14 and 33. Carry amount to **Form 4684** (see instructions) . **35**
36. **Allowable expenses for business use of your home.** Subtract line 35 from line 34. Enter here and on Schedule C, line 30. If your home was used for more than one business, see instructions ▶ **36**

Part III — Depreciation of Your Home

37. Enter the **smaller** of your home's adjusted basis or its fair market value (see instructions) . . . **37**
38. Value of land included on line 37 .... **38**
39. Basis of building. Subtract line 38 from line 37 .... **39**
40. Business basis of building. Multiply line 39 by line 7 .... **40**
41. Depreciation percentage (see instructions) .... **41** %
42. Depreciation allowable (see instructions). Multiply line 40 by line 41. Enter here and on line 30 above **42**

Part IV — Carryover of Unallowed Expenses to 2020

43. Operating expenses. Subtract line 27 from line 26. If less than zero, enter -0- **43**
44. Excess casualty losses and depreciation. Subtract line 33 from line 32. If less than zero, enter -0- . **44**

For Paperwork Reduction Act Notice, see your tax return instructions. Cat. No. 13232M Form **8829** (2019)

The IRS form for Home Office Expense

The total from the 8829 above is then carried to your Schedule C. There is also now a simplified home office expense formula that is easier, where you can take $5 per square foot per year, up to $1,500, and you don't have to worry about any depreciation or other complications. The office worksheet for your use in the forms appendix.

You can take a percentage of your mortgage interest, utilities, and property tax as a deduction on the non-simplified deduction.

You can also expense the portion of your home phone, fax, and internet that you use for business, either using the simplified or long form methods. If your internet, phone, and cable TV are bundled, you'll want to break out the percent you actually use it for business, and deduct that amount only. You ADD these amounts to the general overhead expenses!

An IRS Revenue Agent told me about a case where a taxpayer was audited, and represented herself in the audit (a bad move!). She was self-employed, and claimed her home internet, cable and TV were 100% business, and the IRS agent wasn't willing to let her have that without the taxpayer proving that it was truly all business.

Some personal insults were made to the IRS agent, also. The IRS agent was able to subpoena the internet history from the internet service provider of the taxpayer, and it seemed almost all her internet use was on Facebook, and 'adult' websites and chat rooms. Almost no business at all! She ended up getting a 0% deduction, and a lot of penalties and interest in addition to the tax she would have owed in the first place. The takeaway here is be accurate with your claimed tax deductions on these items, as they can be easily verified for accuracy. And a bigger point: Don't hurl personal insults at an IRS Auditor! They're people, too, and we don't need to give them any *extra* motivation to do their job.

Lying to a Federal agent is a felony under 18 U.S. Code § 1001 and can get you up to 5 years in prison. So don't lie to the IRS.

You can have an office at your real estate business and at your home. The IRS says the office in your home can qualify as your principal place of business for deducting expenses for its use if:
- You use it exclusively and regularly for the administrative or management activities of your trade or business
- You have no other fixed location where you conduct substantial administrative or management activities of your trade or business.

Many real estate agents have a desk that they regularly use at the office, or share a workstation or computer, but they do their real administrative work at their home office. So, if you do your billing, set up appointments via email or phone, receive and or read your business mail and bank statements at home, or pay your business bills at home, rather than at the office where your broker's real estate license resides, you may be able to claim those expenses. You can also deduct your vehicle expenses in traveling to your secondary office -- at the real estate office.

The IRS considers administrative activities to include:

"There are many activities that are administrative or managerial in nature. The following are a few examples.

- Billing customers, clients, or patients.
- Keeping books and records.
- Ordering supplies.
- Setting up appointments.
- Forwarding orders or writing reports."

From *IRS Publication 587 (2017), Business Use of Your Home*

By performing the preceding activities at your home office, you make your home office your administrative office.

If you have a corporation, be aware that the corporation is not allowed to rent your home office from you. But your corporation *is allowed* to reimburse you for your expenses related to your home office expense. Be prepared to show and document that you actually work at home, and it would be a good idea to write on your daily calendar or Outlook calendar times that you work in your home office performing your administrative duties.

Many agents store some of their yard signs in the back of their garage or in a spot in their basement, and want to write off 10% of their household expenses for 'storage' expenses. That doesn't qualify for a real estate agent, as the criteria for storage deduction for business use of the home is quite clear, from

IRS Publication 587 :

*"**Storage of inventory or product samples**. If you use part of your home for storage of inventory or product samples, you can deduct expenses for the business use of your home without meeting the exclusive use test. However, you must meet all the following tests.*
- *You sell products at wholesale or retail as your trade or business.*
- *You keep the inventory or product samples in your home for use in your trade or business.*
- *Your home is the only fixed location of your trade or business.*
- *You use the storage space on a regular basis.*
- *The space you use is a separately identifiable space suitable for storage."*

I read this to some clients, and they say, "Oh yes, that's me!"

No. No, it isn't.

You're not in the business of <u>selling your yard signs</u>. You are in the business of <u>selling real estate</u>. Yard signs are not the inventory of product you sell. They are an ancillary advertising tool, not the product you're selling.

I understand you want to write your garage off as a tax-deductible expense (alas, I would too), but you cannot do so just because you put your yard signs in there. I wish we could make that fly, but remember, your accountant is signing your return *under <u>penalty of perjury</u>* that they did your return *according to the law* as it is; not as we wish it would be. We have clients *VERY UPSET* about this every year – hence the detailed explanation.

The allowable deduction for storage applies to retail inventory, and the IRS gives an example of an individual selling tools directly to the public, and the taxpayer's only location for business is his home. Therefore, he is entitled to deduct costs related to storage of those goods at his home, because his home is essentially his storefront location.

#4 BEST TAX TIP: SECTION 105 MEDICAL PLAN

You may ask, "What good does that do me as a real estate agent with no employees?" I ask: Is there a spouse, child, or close personal friend who helps you (or could be helping you) throughout the year? Read on!

As an employer, you can have one or more employees who works not for a paycheck or wages, but solely for medical benefits. This means no W2 filing requirement for you, the employer, no payroll taxes for you to pay, and less hassle and much less paperwork for an employer such as you.

Using a 105 plan, any reimbursements of employee medical expenses you pay for are tax-deductible and lower your taxable income by that amount. You can hire a child or spouse to do things in your business you don't have the time for or don't want to do. Things like picking up your yard signs, for instance, when they come in those giant 100-lb boxes that are dropped off at the local office.

A 105 plan is very simple and won't take much time to set up.

Your employee (let's say husband) can pick up those 5,000-page reams of paper at the office store for you and bring them to your home office. He can hang around when you do open houses (if you do the anymore) to make sure you're safe and not alone at a strange house when random strangers can pop in unannounced at any time, and maybe not with the intention of buying a house. He may already do all of those things, but now you can legitimately compensate him, and deduct it properly as an expense of doing business.

You can pay your employee's medical expenses as compensation (or pay their out-of-pocket co-pays their primary insurance doesn't pay) instead of paying your employee by the hour. It's not uncommon for a 105-plan arranged like this to reimburse $3,000 a year or more in expenses, all of which are deductible at 100% to the employer (you). The average tax savings we see for our clients that implement a 105 plan is right around $3,000 a year! One client whose spouse had some expensive medical co-pays was able to deduct over $10,000 in the first year alone, which was previously non-deductible!

This arrangement is especially helpful for small businesspeople who may employ spouses, or friends as part-time intermittent helpers that only help you occasionally. <u>A 105 plan works especially well and makes a lot of sense if you have a spouse, domestic partner, or children where you'd end up having to pay the medical bills or co-pays anyway. Now you can write it off!</u> And you can make them do some work to earn it.

You can deduct these payments at 100% through your business, and since most taxpayers cannot deduct much, if any, of their medical expenses because the expenses do not exceed 10% of their Adjusted Gross Income (AGI) for years 2019 and after.

As an example, if you had an AGI (the bottom number on the 1st page of your 1040 tax return) of $100,000, you'd need your unreimbursed medical expenses for you and your spouse to be over $10,000 before even $1 of it would be deductible as an itemized deduction ($10,000 in 2019).

Given the doubling of the standard deduction in 2019, it will be even harder for it to make sense to deduct medical expenses as an itemized deduction, and even then, your real dollar tax savings are only at your incremental tax rate. As a self-employed real estate agent, though, that becomes 100% expensed. How great is that!?

A simple employee agreement could look like this:

> *"Mr. Smith will work for Mrs. Smith and perform various duties as request to assist with Mrs. Smith's real estate business at her direction. His compensation will be in the form of medical reimbursements only. Wages earned are directed to medical expenses. Mr. Smith will submit time sheets every month detailing all worked performed and the hours worked."*

Check with an attorney or accountant in your state, of course, to make sure your employment arrangement is properly set up to comply with your state laws.

Implementing a 105 plan cannot be something you want to run up the flagpole on April 14th of the next year, trying to desperately lower your tax bill at the last minute. You should document the hours worked and the work performed (for any lawyerly types out there that doubt me, see Federal Appeals court case Shellito, et al v. CIR, No. 10-9002 (10th Cir. 2011)), and you, as the employer, should and must be able to document to the IRS that the spouse was indeed an employee and actually performed real work as part of your business.

Our simple layman's summary is that if you hire your spouse, child, or significant other, and you want to deduct their medical expenses as a 100% business expense we recommend you:

1) Have a simple signed employment agreement
2) Keep timecards or time sheets for each period of what specific work and their work hours of what they are doing to earn their pay, just like any other business would, and be able to PROVE they did the work.
3) Have your 105 plan in writing, and you and the spouse/employee should both sign and date it.
4) Follow the plan and document everything thoroughly. Keep the medical bills and cancelled checks or other payment records.

The burden of proof is on the taxpayer, not the government, for tax cases. It wouldn't hurt to have an accountant or attorney help you draw up a plan and to ensure it is properly memorialized at its inception.

An employment contract, for purposes of a 105 plan with a spouse-employee, need not spell out the work hours or specific work duties performed, but simply state that there is an employee-employer relationship and the compensation will be in the form of the medical reimbursement plan.

Time sheets, like the example that follows, will provide necessary documentation that the work was done. Make sure they are filled out every day or week as appropriate.

Time Sheet for Employee

Employee Details:
Manager Details:

Total Work Week Hours   Total Hours Worked

Date(s)	Start Time	End Time	Hours Worked	Work Done

This deduction does not exist for you if you're the employer, just for your employees, and it is not available to S Corp owners for their own bills. The bottom line on the 105, though, is that this may give you the legal ability to write off something at 100% through your business that you might already be paying and cannot currently write off at all.

Now if your employee happens to also be your spouse, and your spouse's dependent children are also your dependent children, that's even better!

PAY YOUR KIDS

You can 'hire' your children as employees to work in your business, and therefore you can deduct their wages from your business income as a business expense.

You generally don't have to withhold or pay any Federal payroll taxes on their wages, if the kids are under 18, although your state or city may have additional employee tax requirements.

Have a signed employment agreement, pay them a paycheck, and track hours worked and what work was done. This allows you to shift part of your business income from your own tax bracket to your child's bracket—which will be much lower than yours. This can result in substantial tax savings. You can use the same simple employment agreement and timesheet as was shown in the previous section on 105 plans. Taxpayers with under $12,000 of earned income don't have to file a tax return, generally.

We have agents who hire their kids to help them clean up yards and houses before showings, drop off literature, clean the home office, wash mom or dad's work car and vacuum it, gather up their staging supplies and props and all sorts of other things. The kids get paid and get some real work experience, earn some money, and mom or dad get a tax deduction!

We have a client who alternatively pays her high school or college age kids to accompany her on open houses, so she's not stuck there alone all day.

Mostly, what happens is Mom or Dad end up giving their kids

spending money throughout the year – lunch money, pizza money, college living expenses, etc. In return for that money, though, the parents get real work in return so that money is *earned* instead of just given and can thereby be lawfully written off by the parents.

MAXIMIZING DEDUCTIONS & STAYING OUT OF TROUBLE WITH THE IRS

We are not going to expand much on accounting for your income in this manual, that part is easy. Well, earning your income can be very hard, but for accounting purposes it is easy for us to get an accurate figure. The company or broker will issue a 1099-MISC that states what the commissions earned for the year were. That's pretty simple math:

Gross sales x commission % = commissions earned

(Gross sales for the year $3 million) x (3% commission) = $90,000

The number one thing we see real estate agent clients miss, yet the most crucial thing, is properly tracking their business expenses.

The first recommendation we make to a new real estate agent client of ours is:

SEPARATE BUSINESS VS. PERSONAL EXPENSES

1: Get a bank account for your realty business only, and use it exclusively for business.

And right behind that is:

<u>2:</u> Keep any business credit card expenses separate from personal credit card expenses.

Keep the statements for both. It's okay if your personal name is on the accounts. That's fine. Just use one for business only.

Keep the monthly statements. The important point is to segregate your personal finances from your business finances. I cannot stress this enough. And keep every receipt for your business expenses!

If real estate agents followed those two very simple rules, it would save an enormous amount of heartache and stress. The failure of many real estate professionals to properly separate business and personal expense records and bank accounts is one reason why IRS agents have a field day when auditing agents.

You likely don't have time every day (or week, or even month) to sort through all the receipts from the grocery store, the office store, your favorite home furnishings store and add up your business expenses – if you mix business and personal items on the same transaction. Keeping separate business accounts will do most of the work for you.

> *A year from now when you're preparing your taxes, there's no way you're going to remember what those items were and what they cost.*

Where do agents go wrong? When you go to the grocery store tonight, and throw in printer paper, envelopes, pens, and other items that are strictly *business* in with the same transaction with a week's worth of family groceries. A year from now when you're preparing your taxes, there's no way you're going to remember what those items were and what they cost and be able to recall the dollar amount of the office supplies vs. the groceries. So maybe you guess, and just come up with a number. Most agents don't keep piles of grocery store receipts or have accountants going through a giant box of receipts with a highlighter and calculator estimating what expenses are business and which are personal. Even if they do, you sure don't want to get the hourly bill for such a colossal waste of time!

It is SO MUCH SIMPLER, AND STRESS-FREE to have one account to deposit your commission checks -- and everything you spend out of it is business expenses, including gas for trips, business meals, your cell phone that clients call you on, and so on.

To 'pay' yourself, just move a chunk of money out of your business and account and put it into your personal account. You don't have to take a certain amount out each month or anything like that. You will still have the complete freedom to move money from your business to personal account at any time.

Moving money from your business account to your personal account is not a taxable event, and you're not taxed on what is in your business or personal bank account at the end of the year.

Your taxable income is going to be your revenues – your expenses. If you close several deals in one month, and you want to take $20,000 out of your business account and put into your personal account to pay for a vacation, go ahead. If you didn't close any sales in a month, you don't have to take any money out. You don't have to make payroll every two weeks and pay yourself a set amount. The purpose of the separate account is solely to make it very easy for you, your accountant, and the IRS to easily and cleanly track your business income and expenses, and very clearly be able to differentiate your personal spending.

Online banking makes it simple (and sometimes free!). Even if you have an S Corp or an LLC, you are taxed on your profit, not on the money leftover in your bank account at the end of the year.

RECORDS YOU MUST KEEP IN CLAIMING TAX DEDUCTIONS

To survive an IRS audit without changes and support the figures shown on a tax return, you will have to keep records that support the business expenses you claim. To be clear, you *can* prepare a tax return without the benefit of any supporting documentation whatsoever, and I've seen returns like that. Its just not proper or necessarily legal to do so. But to sustain deductions, if audited, you must have sufficient documentary evidence to support them, and most especially to document mileage and auto expenses.

In addition to having a business-only bank account, you'll need to be able to provide invoices or cash register receipts that show what items constitute the expense shown on a bank statement.

For instance, we just cannot just show an IRS agent a $145 debit card charge from a store on a bank statement and sustain that deduction as a business expense. We'll need the cash register receipt that shows exactly what that legitimate business expense was.

For real estate agents who get audited, the IRS will generally want to see:
- Your 1099s, W2s and other income documents
- your appointment book (or a printout of your Outlook or other online calendar)
- a copy of all your listings for the year
- your daily mileage log (which had better match the entries on your appointment book)
- Copies of your bank and credit card statements

- Supporting documentation for all expenses

By retaining all these documents and information, you will have a nearly bullet-proof toolkit to use in case you get audited by the IRS. We do a lot of audit defense at our sister company Tax Defense Ohio, and have seen very few cases where an IRS officer will ask for every receipt for a taxpayer for the entire tax year. It has happened, and if they indeed ask, you must have the documentation to sustain your deduction. Frequently they are okay with bank and credit card statements, as long as the transactions seem to be for business purposes.

Documentation you should keep to prove expenses includes:
- Bank Statements
- Cash register receipts
- Credit Card Statements
- Sales invoices
- Receipts for meals & travel

Attention: What you paid for this book is tax deductible!

What follows is one of the forms we give to clients to show them the various expenses, and this is a no-frills affair straight from our tax software. The client can go through her records and fill-in-the-blanks with the totals for each line or let us do the math. The result is the same: every bit of the allowable expense is accounted for, which lowers the tax liability and lets you keep more of your money.

Not all these items line up exactly with what is shown on the Schedule C, and several of the items on the following page will be added up and put into one line-item. There's one sheet for general expenses, and the second sheet is specific to automobile and travel expenses. This form works fine if you have an S Corp or LLC, too. EXPENSES:

Sales Related Expenses	
Advertising	
Appraisal Fees	
Business Cards	
Clerical	
Client Gifts	
Courier Service	
Commissions paid	
Referral Fees	
Cards/Flowers	
Keys/lockbox	
Maps & books	
Office Expense	
Open House	
Rent	
Sales Assistants	
Repairs	
Signage	
Meals	
Software	
Copies	
printing	
Other	
Staging, drones, etc.	
Total	

Professional	
Professional Dues	
EGO insurance	
Legal Fees	
Accounting Fees	
Lienees	
Membership	
MLS	
Centralized Showing	
Publications	
Seminars	
Continuing Education	
Other	
Communications	
Cell Phone	
Internet	
Fax service	
Other	
Office Equipment	
Computer	
Desk	
Office furniture	
Other	
Other	
Total	

VEHICLE EXPENSES

(Use one for each car)

Vehicle Expenses	
Description of Vehicle	
Date Placed in Service	
Beginning odometer mileage	
Ending odometer mileage	
Total miles	
Business Miles	
Commute Miles	
Personal Miles	
Leased car?	Y / N ?
Was car depreciated in prior tax year?	Y / N ?
Gasoline Expense	
Oil, car washes, etc.	
Repair & Maintenance	
Tires	
Towing / AAA	
Other	
Purchase price	
Sales tax paid	
Annual vehicle tax	

Vehicle Expenses	
Insurance	
License Tags	
Property Tax	
Lease payments	
Car loan interest	
Warranty costs	
Other	
Other	
Car sold during tax year?	Y / N ?
Travel & Expenses	
Airfare	
Car rental, gas	
Parking	
Tolls	
Lodging	
Meals	
Days out of town	
Total	

IRS MILEAGE / AUTO EXPENSE AUDITS

You can go back to your bank or credit card statements and add the numbers up for the year. Write the totals on the sheet and put them in the right places on your tax return or give the summaries to your accountant.

> *Don't want to track mileage every day in an annoying little book? Don't! Get an app like MileIQ or Quickbooks and let it do the work for you!*

Not everything shown on either of these expense sheets will apply to everyone, but it gives a very good example of the range of items that may be deducted. For clients who keep good records, we will go through actual cost of owning and operating your car versus mileage and calculate which method is more advantageous to the taxpayer. You can deduct a fixed cost per business mile driven (58 cents per mile for your 2019 tax return that you'll file in 2020) or the actual cost of the car, gas, insurance, tires, etc. multiplied by your business use percentage of the vehicle.

One item of importance is that when real estate agents get audited by the IRS, the most common deduction category we see examined is the mileage and automobile expense.

You must be able to document every expenditure on your tax return in order to deduct it on your taxes. Now, that doesn't mean your accountant will make you 'prove' you really drove 20,000 miles last year to put it on your tax return. You can bet that the engagement  letter you signed indicated that the tax preparer takes no responsibility for the figures you furnish, and that you are attesting your expenses you gave him are truthful and accurate.

If you should get audited by the IRS (examined, in their parlance) you may be required to document and prove each and every mile you claimed as an expense. In my experience, maybe half our clients truly have no idea how much they drove for business purposes; they kind of guess. They certainly don't log every appointment every day.

We've had cases where clients prepared their own tax returns, and then got audited a year or two later. The IRS requests a daily mileage log – of where the taxpayer went, every day, that is supposed to add up to the number of miles or automobile expense being claimed. And we've had to go back from emails, Outlook calendars, MLS listing dates, Centralized Showing System records and more, just to try to put something together to justify the mileage the client claimed on their tax return. We will make a spreadsheet showing the mileage each day, as best we can determine, based off all those records. We've had to hand a client a bill for $3,000 for this work. Granted, that is a lot better than paying the $11,000 extra in taxes, penalties, and interest. But it would be much easier, far less expensive and a lot less stressful to just keep the appropriate records in the first place!

Let me give you a hint, and please highlight this: You did not drive 20,000 miles for business last year. I have no idea why so many people think this is the magic number, but it can get you in serious trouble with the IRS! You are signing a tax return under penalty of *perjury*. **It's a felony – more than 1 year in prison – to lie on your tax return.** And your tax return preparer is signing it too, and believe me, he or she is not going to jail to save you a couple hundred or thousand bucks.

Back to the mileage documentation: You didn't drive exactly 20,000 miles. You may have driven 19,423 or 22,656. I probably have 20 new clients every year who all insist, pledge, and promise they drove 20,000 miles exactly when I first ask them.

Yes, it takes a little work to track your business miles. Yes, its required by law if you want to deduct automobile expenses.

The moral of the story is - track the drive to each showing, every trip to the post office, and everywhere else -- in some appointment or calendar tracking app on your cell phone, or in an old-fashioned paper notebook.

You need to not only show your business miles, but also your personal miles, so that they can be differentiated. A sample page from our mileage log is as follows:

REALTY INCOME TAX ADVISORS

Simple Mileage Log
Date_____

Appointment	Who/Where/Why	Miles	Business/Personal	
8:00				
9:00				
10:00				
11:00				
12:00				
1:00				
2:00				
3:00				
4:00				
5:00				
6:00				
7:00				
8:00				

Business miles total: _____
Personal miles total: _____

Ending Odometer: _____

You don't need a paper form filled out like this, but you do need all this information. Keep it electronically if you like.

Even if you use actual cost instead of mileage, you still have to prove your percentage of business use, which is still based on miles driven. So if you say the total cost of your Lexus was $10,000 last year, and you used it 70% for business, you better be able to come up with figures that accurately prove you drove 70% business, 30% personal. <u>Estimates and guesses will not do</u>. So, you are back to tracking mileage. And yes, again, you do need this level of detail to sustain your deduction. The closest thing to estimating you can legally do is track 3 straight months and apply that ratio of mileage to the entire year.

According to the *Internal Revenue Service Data Book, 2017,* tax returns with business income, like those filed by <u>real estate agents</u>, are examined (audited) by the IRS on a rate of 1.9-2.1% depending on the income range. It follows that you'd basically have a 1-in-50 chance of getting audited, just looking at the numbers. In my experience who seems to get audited most often are business owners and other taxpayers with a enormous amount of deductible mileage and other expenses.

No matter what the audit odds, though, tax laws should be 100% complied with in all cases. The penalties and long-term consequences drastically outweigh any temporary short-term advantages a taxpayer may think exists by 'fudging' some numbers.

A perfect mileage log that will get you a 100% deduction, every time, with every IRS agent in country is as simple as the example on the previous page and takes all of 10 seconds per entry. Many clients complain out this, but hey, I didn't write the law, and you and I are both stuck with it! You want to claim the deduction? You have to document your claims. Keep gas and repair receipts, too, and you're bullet-proof.

Also, if you go to the post office or the office supply store, you will keep the receipts 1) to show your deduction for those expenses, and 2) since it helps substantiate your mileage deduction. Your receipt from the office store helps support your mileage log entry for the same date, and vice versa.

Clients sometimes bristle when I tell them to keep a mileage log. I've attached a picture of mine, below, that shows essentially all the information on the sheets on the previous pages, but it's a 3 x 4-inch notebook that I got at the office store for 80 cents. Now that I look at it, it's kind of embarrassing, and I am not particularly proud of it, yet it keeps me in compliance with the recordkeeping requirements of the law and lets me maximize my deductions.

> **Harsh Truth: You DO have 30 seconds a day to fill in a mileage log if you have 30 *minutes* a day to play on your phone**

I buy 4 or 5 at a time and keep it in the console of my car (yes, that is a coffee stain, too!). The "B" column is business, "P" is personal. Yes, my handwriting is horrible, but I can readily translate the scratchings below into English to prepare my taxes, or to explain the entries to an IRS agent. Yes, I actually fill it out every day.

A classy, sophisticated actual mileage log
Photo courtesy of author

It takes 30 seconds to fill in. With how much time the average American spends with their head stuck over their phone playing games, or wasting time on Facebook, I'm just not at all sympathetic to the argument that *"I just don't have time."* You have 30 seconds a day to fill in a mileage log if you have 30 *minutes* to play on Facebook.

You have the time, because you are serious enough about your finances to get this manual and implement our system. Just this step can save you several thousand dollars a year –many thousands if you get audited!

METHODS FOR MAXIMIZING YOUR MILEAGE DEDUCTIONS

The preceding material discussed how to document the miles you drive now; this section will address methods <u>to build more **deductible business miles** into your tax return.</u> The more you drive, of course, the more you can write off. As we've said, commuting mileage is not deductible to your regular and ordinary office, like if your main office is at your real estate company's office every day and have a desk there.

The IRS would consider regular work locations as any place where you perform work or services on a regular basis. A temporary work location is usually defined by the IRS as a work location for one year or less.

Those commuting mile rules do not apply, though<u>, if your home office is your regular work office</u> and you drive to a temporary work location, like the Re/Max or Century 21 office on occasion. You can write off a lot more mileage with this one little change!

You would also be able to deduct mileage from your home to a showing, or your home to pick up business cards, office store, bank or any other work-related location that is not strictly commuting.

To maximize your mileage deductions (legally!) you could leave from your Home Office and travel to a meeting with a client, or check your post office box. Then stop by the grocery store or to pick up your kids on the way back from that meeting, thereby making much or <u>all the return mileage</u> back as <u>deductible</u> business mileage.

The idea is to try to maximize how you 'line up' as many personal stops as easily practicable on the way to your business trips, making your personal mileage as negligible as possible and taking the most business mileage, and expense, as you can.

MILEAGE VS. ACTUAL EXPENSE

Many clients elect to just deduct their mileage because it is a little simpler to track than trying to document all the expenses that would add up to the actual cost. Self-employed taxpayers can deduct the cost of interest on car loans, for the business use portion, and this fact is frequently overlooked.

If you take a look at the vehicle expense sheet a few pages ago, you can deduct depreciation, repairs, maintenance, car washes, gas, insurance, parking, tolls, and license fees.

You can also deduct sales tax on the cost of the car. So a $25,000 car would have a sales tax bill of $1,875 attached to it in an area with a 7.5% sales tax.

BUSINESS MEALS

Meals expenses for business is a subject that a lot of people *intentionally* confuse. According to the IRS, you must have records to prove the business purpose and the amount of each expense, the date and place of the business meal, and the business relationship of the persons. These meals can be with current or potential clients, or referral sources. For our purposes, the default reason for business meals is to pursue future business.

We see clients come in every year with their Starbucks or Panera Bread receipts clearly showing a coffee and a muffin, for 200+ days a year, and they get mad when I tell them they cannot legitimately write off their own lunch and coffee everyday as a business expense when they didn't meet with or discuss business with anyone else.

Generally, only 50% of business-related meal expenses are allowed as a deduction.

PLEASE NOTE: The Tax Cuts and Jobs act of 2018 killed off the entertainment deduction, so you can no longer deduct golf, skiing, tickets to concerts, football, hockey, baseball games, theatre, etc. for tax years 2018 and on.

For meals, I recommend clients write the name of the person they met with, and the purpose of the meal, on the back of the receipt. Keep it. Your return will be prepared based on your expense sheets, Excel, QuickBooks, or business bank or credit card statements (see how easy this is going to be now with your business and personal accounts separated?)

You don't need to give your accountant the receipt, but keep it in case you are audited. We really don't want to go through every receipt you had for the whole year, and I would bill you for every minute of my time if you made me do it – I'll bet your accountant will too!

For meal expenses, you need to document, at the time or around the time of the meeting:
- Who you met with
- Where you met
- Why you met (to produce future business!)

PRESENTATIONS VS. BUSINESS MEALS

In an IRS private letter ruling, a real estate agent provided free meals as part of a presentation he gave to sales prospects who attended. The IRS found that unlike normal business meals, these presentations were in fact 100% deductible since the presenter himself and his employees were not participants in the dinner.

He found these prospects from drawings and telemarking, and they had to sit through a sales presentation after the meal. The difference here is that the food and entertainment expense is entirely for the benefit of the potential client, and not for the business owner himself, so he could write it off at 100%.

My firm, for instance, gives tax presentations to real estate agents and we frequently end up buying pizzas, or bagels and carafes of coffee, and we write off every penny. But one of us is up at the front of the room with the PowerPoint clicker, and another staff member or two are working the room, manning the sign-in sheet, filling out continuing education forms or other paperwork.

ESTIMATED TAXES

Since real estate agents don't get a regular paycheck with withholdings, they usually have to make estimated tax payments.

Estimated tax is required not only for your regular income tax, but other taxes such as self-employment tax and alternative minimum tax, which are also calculated on your 1040. If you don't pay enough tax through withholding (such as on a W2) and estimated tax payments, you may be charged a penalty by the IRS. You also may be charged a penalty if your estimated tax payments are late, even if you are due a refund when you file your tax return.

The big problem with this method is that you don't sell houses equally throughout the four quarters of the year. Real estate agents may close three sales in one month, and then go four months with none.

This irregular income stream can make it very hard to keep a household budget in order, much less pay the IRS. The more compelling reason to send in estimated payments whenever you close a sale is so you're actually paying tax when you have to money to do so. We see taxpayers every year that did very well selling all year long, only to be stuck the next April with a $30,000 tax bill they cannot now pay because they spent everything they earned.

We recommend a much simpler and much easier to follow method of paying estimated taxes for real estate agents, and that is to simply send the IRS a check every time you get a commission. You simply take the amount of each commission check and send the IRS an estimated tax payment for that amount.

So if you closed a $200,000 property, and got a $6,000 check, we will tell you that from last year we expect you to be in the 22% bracket, send the IRS $1,320.

$$\$6,000 \times .22 = \$1,320$$

We prepare the blank estimated payment coupons, give them to the client with instructions, and this way you are only making estimated tax payments when you have the money to do so. See page 165 for the vouchers, and a printable copy is on your Forms & Publications CD. Depending upon what state you live in, there is a different IRS center to send your estimated payments. The principal works for state income taxes, too.

You avoid an estimated tax penalty if you either owe less than $1,000 in tax after subtracting any estimates, withholdings, and refundable credits. You also avoid it if you paid withholding and estimated tax of at least 90% of the tax for the current year, or 100% of the tax shown on the return for the prior year.

If you set up as an S Corp, you can have federal tax withheld on your paychecks and reflected on your W2 in amounts sufficient so that you'll no longer have to make quarterly estimates. That's much more convenient that than having to write a giant check every three months.

Record of Estimated Tax Payments (Farmers, fishermen, and fiscal year taxpayers, see *Payment Due Dates*.)

Keep for Your Records

Payment number	Payment due date	(a) Amount due	(b) Date paid	(c) Check or money order number, or credit or debit card confirmation number	(d) Amount paid (do not include any convenience fee)	(e) 2018 overpayment credit applied	(f) Total amount paid and credited (add (d) and (e))
1	4/15/2019						
2	6/17/2019						
3	9/16/2019						
4	1/15/2020*						
Total				▶			

* You do not have to make this payment if you file your 2019 tax return by January 31, 2020, **and** pay the entire balance due with your return.

Privacy Act and Paperwork Reduction Act Notice. We ask for this information to carry out the tax laws of the United States. We need it to figure and collect the right amount of tax. Our legal right to ask for this information is Internal Revenue Code section 6654, which requires that you pay your taxes in a specified manner to avoid being penalized. Additionally, sections 6001, 6011, and 6012(a) and their regulations require you to file a return or statement for any tax for which you are liable; section 6109 requires you to provide your identifying number. Failure to provide this information, or providing false or fraudulent information, may subject you to penalties.

You are not required to provide the information requested on a form that is subject to the Paperwork Reduction Act unless the form displays a valid OMB control number. Books or records relating to a form or its instructions must be retained as long as their contents may become material in the administration of any Internal Revenue law. Generally, tax returns and return information are confidential, as stated in Code section 6103.

We may disclose the information to the Department of Justice for civil and criminal litigation and to other federal agencies, as provided by law.

We may disclose it to cities, states, the District of Columbia, and U.S. commonwealths or possessions to carry out their tax laws. We may also disclose this information to other countries under a tax treaty, to federal and state agencies to enforce federal nontax criminal laws, or to federal law enforcement and intelligence agencies to combat terrorism.

If you do not file a return, do not give the information asked for, or give fraudulent information, you may be charged penalties and be subject to criminal prosecution.

Please keep this notice with your records. It may help you if we ask you for other information. If you have any questions about the rules for filing and giving information, please call or visit any Internal Revenue Service office.

The average time and expenses required to complete and file this form will vary depending on individual circumstances. For the estimated averages, see the instructions for your income tax return.

If you have suggestions for making this package simpler, we would be happy to hear from you. See the instructions for your income tax return.

Tear off here

Form **1040-ES** | Department of the Treasury — Internal Revenue Service | **2019 Estimated Tax** | **Payment Voucher 4** | OMB No. 1545-0074

Calendar year—Due Jan. 15, 2020

File only if you are making a payment of estimated tax by check or money order. Mail this voucher with your check or money order payable to "**United States Treasury**." Write your social security number and "2019 Form 1040-ES" on your check or money order. Do not send cash. Enclose, but do not staple or attach, your payment with this voucher.

Amount of estimated tax you are paying by check or money order. | Dollars | Cents

Pay online at www.irs.gov/epay
Simple. Fast. Secure.

Print or type:
- Your first name and initial | Your last name | Your social security number
- If joint payment, complete for spouse
- Spouse's first name and initial | Spouse's last name | Spouse's social security number
- Address (number, street, and apt. no.)
- City, state, and ZIP code. (If a foreign address, enter city, also complete spaces below.)
- Foreign country name | Foreign province/county | Foreign postal code

For Privacy Act and Paperwork Reduction Act Notice, see instructions.

Form **1040-ES** (2019)

-9-

Estimated tax voucher, form 1040ES

55

HEALTH INSURANCE FOR THE SELF-EMPLOYED

Self-employed individuals who file a Schedule C can generally deduct their health insurance expenses on the front page of their 1040. The deduction allows self-employed people to reduce their adjusted gross income by the amount they pay in health insurance premiums, and goes on line 29 of the 1040 (on the 2017 tax year 1040).

It's a little more complicated for individuals who are more than 2% owners of an S Corp, however, the taxpayer must do the following:

- The S corporation must pay for your insurance premiums, either directly or through reimbursement
- The premiums paid for the health insurance must be shown as wages on box 1 of your W2 (not box 3 or 5, so there is no self-employment tax on it)
- Then you as the S Corp owner would deduct the cost on page 1 of your Form 1040.

QUALIFIED SMALL BUSINESS HEALTH REIMBURSEMENT ARRANGEMENT

As of January 1, 2017, you can implement a qualified small employer health reimbursement arrangement (QSEHRA) and start helping your employees pay for their health insurance and other medical costs, without worrying about the per-employee $100-a-day penalty from the Affordable Care Act ($36,500 per employee per year). This applies only to real estate agents and brokers (or other businesses) with employees.

With this new plan, your eligible small business can reimburse individually purchased health insurance and other deductible medical costs of up to $4,950 for an individual and up to $10,000 for a family for tax year 2018.

You need to give your employees written notice of the qualified small employer health reimbursement arrangement as follows:

- Ninety days before the beginning of a plan year (for calendar years 2018 and later)
- In the case of an employee who is not eligible to participate in the arrangement as of the beginning of a plan year, the date on which such employee is first eligible

The written notice to the eligible employees needs to state:

- The amount of the employee's permitted benefit for the year,
- That the employee should provide the information about the permitted benefit to any health insurance exchange to which the employee applies for advance payment of the premium assistance tax credit, and
- A warning that if the employee is not covered under minimum essential coverage for any month, the employee may be subject to tax under section 500A, for such month and reimbursements under the arrangement may be includable in gross income (even though President Trump suspended the collection of the Penalty administratively).

The new law states that after the employee provides proof of minimum essential coverage, the employer may pay or reimburse the eligible employee for medical expenses defined in IRC Section 213(d) that were or are incurred by the eligible employee and, in the case of a family plan, his or her family members.

To protect yourself and meet the letter of the law, you can use a reimbursement form that requires the employee to provide proof of minimum essential coverage and attestation with respect to requests for any Section 213(d) reimbursements or payments. This is allowed only for small employers with less than 50 employees.

CASHING IN ON THE TAX CUTS AND JOBS ACT CHANGES

Although this should be old news to most self employed individuals, the Tax Cuts and Jobs Act of 2018 is having significant impact on small businesses, like most real estate agents. There are new agents just starting out in real estate every day, making the change from a W2 job, and they need to know about the TCJA.

The important fact for you is that the law generally provides a <u>20 percent deduction for pass-through businesses!</u> And that's on top of the roughly 2% tax cut that went into effect when all the marginal tax rates went down on January 1, 2018.

Taxpayers who file Schedule C claim the 20 percent deduction if their taxable income is under $157,500 for single filers or $315,000 for joint filers, and this also applies to owners or shareholders of partnerships, some types of LLCs, and S-Corps. This is huge, and has been almost completely ignored by the media! This is the biggest benefit to self-employed and small businesspeople ever in the tax code.

In simple terms, in a comparison from 2017 to 2018 (and later) tax codes, if you made a $100,000 taxable income in 2017, you would pay an equal income tax to what you'd pay with a $125,000 income in 2018!

This volume is being finished in December 2019 and the law is still in effect. This is for income tax only and does not address self-employment tax.

This tax deduction is already in the law, and there's no action you must take to take advantage of it.

CHOICE OF BUSINESS ENTITY

Most real estate agents file their taxes as sole proprietors, which means they are someone who owns an unincorporated business as the sole owner. You and your business are the same legal entity, and you file a Schedule C on your 1040 tax return to report your business activity.

Despite the common misconception, just paying your state a $75 filing fee and putting "LLC" on the end of your business name does not make it a separate business entity and legally remove you from the business tax liabilities with the IRS. It's still just you, and you are filing taxes on your 1040.

There are both legal and tax factors that are critical to your selection of a business entity. The first consideration is liability – and we are talking about limited liability companies here. By placing your business activities inside an LLC that is a separate legal entity from you, you're building a legal wall around your personal assets and protecting them from lawsuits and other actions that may arise against the business.

Say you have a rental property in your LLC name, and your tenant gets drunk and falls down the stairs and breaks his arm. The rental contract is made out to the LLC name, the rent checks are made out to the LLC name, and therefore he's going to have a tougher time suing you and securing a judgement against your personal assets.

If you were to continue operation of your real estate ventures in your own personal name, your personal assets would be much more exposed to legal liability. For a real estate agent, it might be a seller threatening to sue you because their house didn't sell, or for a fair housing discrimination suit.

The idea is that if something bad were to happen, and the runaway jury decided the drunk tenant needed that $2 million for wine and lottery tickets, if the LLC were to be found liable, the extent of its liability would be the assets it owns. Hence the limited liability company name. It's sort of similar to the manner in which shareholders in a large C Corporation such as Wal-Mart are not all personally liable for any debts owed by Wal-Mart; their only money at risk is the amounts they have invested in the company.

The LLC filing structure offers much improved liability protection with very simple tax filing options. If you file a Schedule C, you just ignore your LLC for purposes of filing your Federal taxes. You will file your self-employment taxes on a Schedule SE, and you'll generally have to make estimated tax payments. LLCs filing Schedule C do not issue their single-owners a W2, so no payroll taxes are withheld as would be the case for a normal employee. It is very simple compared to having corporation or partnership.

You'll find that high-income earning LLC owners who file a Schedule C pay the maximum amount of self-employment tax a person can pay. This can be cut substantially with a S Corp structure.

Note that an LLC or Corporate structure will not save you from being sued personally for errors or omissions, malpractice, or torts. So, if your attorney made a glaring mistake on your Dad's will and it cost you $20 million, you very likely still have a case against him even if he's part of an LLC or other entity, because *he personally* did the work or made the error.

Where the LLC helps is general business liabilities such as a shopper slipping on the sidewalk, or a customer trying to sue you personally because your delivery driver plowed your company van through his landscaping and into his pool. You need to still have liability insurance and take other prudent business measures just as you did before, LLCs offer another level of protection.

That same logic holds true with the LLC and it makes a tremendous amount of sense as a stop-loss measure for your realty activities. The LLC *needs* to be *run* as a *separate* legal entity from you. As we've said a lot in this manual, have a separate bank account for the company. If you deposit checks for the LLC into your personal account, or vice versa, you can jeopardize your LLC 'corporate veil'. If you have an LLC, get a separate tax ID for it, and operate it separately from your personal affairs.

Once you decide you want the advantages of limited liability and you want an LLC, you need to choose how the entity will file its taxes.

Notice that we didn't mention the filing of an LLC tax return. There is no "LLC Tax Return". An LLC can file its tax return in one of three ways:
1. As a Single Member LLC on your 1040 (schedule C for your self-employment income, schedule E for rentals, as we discussed above)
2. As a partnership filing a Form 1065 tax return. You need two or more business owners to file a tax return as a partnership.
3. As an LLC electing to be taxed as an S Corporation, filing a Form 1120S tax return.

If you're the only owner of your business, you can file as a Schedule C proprietorship, as an S Corp, or as a C Corp.

GENERAL S CORP FORMATION QUALIFICATIONS

To qualify for S corporation status, the corporation must meet the following requirements:

- Be a domestic corporation (incorporated in the United States)
- Have only allowable shareholders
- May be individuals, certain trusts, and estates and
- May not be partnerships, corporations or non-resident alien shareholders
- Have no more than 100 shareholders
- Have only one class of stock
- Not be an ineligible corporation (i.e. certain financial institutions, insurance companies, and domestic international sales corporations).

Most every sole practitioner real estate agent in the country would thereby meet the general qualifications to set up their business as an S Corp.

A K-1 is shown on the next page, it's the form that shows the pass-through items from your S Corp to your personal tax return.

Schedule K-1 (Form 1120-S)

Department of the Treasury
Internal Revenue Service

For calendar year 2019, or tax year

beginning __/__/2019 ending __/__/__

2019

☐ Final K-1   ☐ Amended K-1   OMB No. 1545-0123

671119

Shareholder's Share of Income, Deductions, Credits, etc.
▶ See back of form and separate instructions.

Part I — Information About the Corporation

A. Corporation's employer identification number

B. Corporation's name, address, city, state, and ZIP code

C. IRS Center where corporation filed return

Part II — Information About the Shareholder

D. Shareholder's identifying number

E. Shareholder's name, address, city, state, and ZIP code

F. Shareholder's percentage of stock ownership for tax year . . . . _____ %

For IRS Use Only

Part III — Shareholder's Share of Current Year Income, Deductions, Credits, and Other Items

#	Item	#	Item
1	Ordinary business income (loss)	13	Credits
2	Net rental real estate income (loss)		
3	Other net rental income (loss)		
4	Interest income		
5a	Ordinary dividends		
5b	Qualified dividends	14	Foreign transactions
6	Royalties		
7	Net short-term capital gain (loss)		
8a	Net long-term capital gain (loss)		
8b	Collectibles (28%) gain (loss)		
8c	Unrecaptured section 1250 gain		
9	Net section 1231 gain (loss)		
10	Other income (loss)	15	Alternative minimum tax (AMT) items
11	Section 179 deduction	16	Items affecting shareholder basis
12	Other deductions		
		17	Other information

18. ☐ More than one activity for at-risk purposes*
19. ☐ More than one activity for passive activity purposes*

* See attached statement for additional information.

For Paperwork Reduction Act Notice, see the Instructions for Form 1120-S.   www.irs.gov/Form1120S   Cat. No. 11520D   Schedule K-1 (Form 1120-S) 2019

Form K1 From the S Corp

You will want to set up a business bank account for the S Corp, unless you already had an LLC and you keep the same name.

> **EVERYONE SAYS THEY HAVE AN LLC, NOBODY REALLY KNOWS WHAT IT MEANS.** –
> *Overheard at a local Realtor© meeting*

"Everyone says they have an LLC, nobody really knows what it means." That's a funny line we heard while giving a presentation to a large group of real estate agents, and it's funny because it's so very true. Just setting up the LLC with your state does nothing for you.

The Tax Reform and Jobs Act, and the 20% the pass-thru taxation changes in Section 199A do not reduce the self-employment tax savings of an S Corp. The additional pass-thru deduction will help taxpayers even more with the benefits of an S corporation.

S CORP DRAWBACKS

There are some disadvantages or drawbacks to having your real estate business set up as an S Corp, most of which we have already addressed:

- You will have more paperwork to do, specifically a W2/payroll taxes and a file 1120S S Corp tax return annually
- You'll have to file 941 payroll reports each quarter, and 940 annual Federal unemployment reports
- There may be state or city tax filing requirements and tax obligations as well
- Some states such as California, New York, and Tennessee have their own specific additional filing requirements

RETROACTIVE S CORP ELECTION

The IRS has Revenue Procedures (Rev Procs in CPA talk) that are available where taxpayers under certain circumstances can retroactively go back in time and still get the advantage of saving self-employment taxes if you have a business entity set up already.

There are several other details, but most self-employed people with an LLC will qualify – and you'll probably need an accountant to help, but if it saves you $10,000 or more, won't it be worth it?

One Rev Proc we use allows business owners to elect S Corp Status within 3 years and 75 days late, but they must have been operating as an S Corp and paying themselves like an S Corp on their tax returns for those years. You can use Rev. Proc. 2013-30, and it grants late relief by consolidating numerous other revenue procedures into one revenue procedure and extending relief in certain circumstances.

For S corporation elections, the corporate classification election goes back to the date you <u>intended</u> the S Corp to take effect, up to 3 years and 75 days of the effective date of the election.

Usually, the relief under Rev. Proc. 2013-30 is approved by the IRS when the company does not qualify solely because it failed to file the 2553 timely or accurately with the applicable IRS office, and all returns reported income consistently as if the election was in effect.

We have had several cases like this where clients had failed to file a 2553 correctly, and had all their 1120S returns rejected by the IRS.

The IRS will then accrue penalties and interest on the 1120C return that was never actually filed! Using Rev. Proc. 2013-30 can save you in this case, under many circumstances.

The IRS has published a guide that details who qualifies for late election relief, and Rev. Proc. 2013-30 includes flow charts, as well as specific guidance for super-detailed instructions on how to do this.

If you do not qualify for relief under Rev. Proc. 2013-30, you can request relief by requesting a private letter ruling with the IRS, which requires professional assistance.

To get your S Corp late election accepted, you may have to go back and file a W2 and W3, or maybe a 1099-MISC, and any state payroll tax returns for the past tax years. Some folks issue a 1099 to themselves from the S Corp for the late years, instead. It depends on your facts and circumstances which way works out best.

C CORPORATIONS MAKE A COMEBACK – KIND OF

The Jobs and Tax Cuts Act of 2018 did help out C Corps quite a bit, as the tax rate fell to 21% for the corporation, where it had been 35% before. Owners of the C Corp get paid W2 wages, and the corporation itself is also taxed (unlike an LLC filing as a Sched C, 1065 or as an S Corp) so there is still double taxation in a C Corp.

C Corporations are required to have annual corporate meetings under most state organizing laws, and may have additional annual filing requirements.

C Corps really fell out of favor for small businesses due to the double taxation, but 2018 *may* be the year they are poised to make a comeback. Business losses to not flow through back to your personal return, but the corporation can carry back losses 2 years and carry them forward 20 years. There is no payroll tax savings like those available to S Corp owners.

C Corporations can also pay their shareholders dividends, which are taxed to the owners. C Corps are taxed directly and pay income taxes with their form 1120. S Corps pass on their income tax liability attributes to their owners, and the *owners* pay the income taxes.

COMMON TAX MYTHS THAT CAN GET YOU INTO TROUBLE

- *Myth: "I bought a magnetic sticker and put it on my car, so I'm always advertising with it, therefore all my car expenses are 100% deductible."* **Fact:** That's a commonly heard myth, but it just isn't true. Your personal mileage is still personal, and only your business usage would actually be deductible, just like in a vehicle with no sign.

- *Myth: "My car is really my office, so I can write off everything related to it!"*
  Fact: Your car is not an office, and just because you make phone calls from your car, it doesn't in any way transform your personal miles into business. Everyone with a phone and a car makes calls from their car. Don't think that legally makes it an office.

> Everyone with a phone and a car makes calls from their car. Don't think that legally makes it an office.

- *"Myth: I don't need to have a mileage log, because I claim a percentage of business use."*
  Fact: This isn't true, as we pointed out in the section on mileage. If you claim automobile expense in any manner, you need to prove where you went, when, and why. Only a mileage log meets the criteria the IRS has established for corroborating evidence.

- *Myth: "I can write off my lunch everyday as long as I am at work or if I even talk to someone on the phone or email them about a work-related matter."*

    Fact: If you claim too many lunches or dinners, in the judgement of the IRS, they can assert that you are having too many meals and therefore expensing through your business what are really personal expenses. We see this more than a dozen times a year, where clients present us with some preposterously high figure as their meal expense, and a couple hundred drive-thru receipts for one person. *Sutter v. Commissioner* is the IRS case that most accountants will reference.

- *Myth: "I can write off season tickets to my hometown football team or local performing arts, etc. if I take clients to some events."*

    Fact: You used to be able partially deduct amounts that would accrue to each separate game, for business use. The Tax Cuts and Jobs Act of 2017 effectively eliminated the entertainment deduction, however.

- *Myth: "I can write off my profession clothing – I only wear that suit, or those shoes – for work, so it is work expense and I can write it off."*

    Fact: Clothing that you buy that is suitable for everyday wear – such as suits, dress pants or slacks, shoes or whatever – is not tax deductible. Even if you only wear it to work. The only type of clothing you can expense for tax purposes is that which is not suitable for everyday wear – such as a fireman's uniform, police uniform, nurse and doctor scrubs, fire retardant clothing that steelworkers may use, etc. Dry cleaning is likewise not deductible.

Designer Clothes Are NOT Deductible! (nor are your regular clothes)

- ***Myth: "I don't make enough money to get audited. The IRS is really only concerned about big-time Wall Street tax cheats."***

    Fact: The IRS does audit high-income earners at a higher rate, but you can be audited at random for no reason, or selected for an examination based on DIF score criteria. DIF scores base the potential for audit findings based on returns filed with similar income/expense/deduction criteria. If you claim you made $40,000 last year, but your mortgage interest and property taxes were $25,000 – you can see how that might look a little off to the IRS or anyone else looking at a tax return.

From IRS Publication 556:
"How Returns Are Selected for Examination

The IRS selects returns using a variety of methods, including:

Potential participants in abusive tax avoidance transactions — Some returns are selected based on information obtained by the IRS through efforts to identify promoters and participants of abusive tax avoidance transactions. Examples include information received from "John Doe" summonses issued to credit card companies and businesses and participant lists from promoters ordered by the courts to be turned over to the IRS.

Computer Scoring — Some returns are selected for examination on the basis of computer scoring. Computer programs give each return numeric "scores". The Discriminant Function System (DIF) score rates the potential for change, based on past IRS experience with similar returns. The Unreported Income DIF (UIDIF) score rates the return for the potential of unreported income. IRS personnel screen the highest-scoring returns, selecting some for audit and identifying the items on these returns that are most likely to need review.

Large Corporations — The IRS examines many large corporate returns annually.

Information Matching — Some returns are examined because payer reports, such as Forms W-2 from employers or Form 1099 interest statements from banks, do not match the income reported on the tax return.

Related Examinations — Returns may be selected for audit when they involve issues or transactions with other taxpayers, such as business partners or investors, whose returns were selected for examination.

'Other — Area offices may identify returns for examination in connection with local compliance projects. These projects require higher level management approval and deal with areas such as local compliance initiatives, return preparers or specific market segments."

- **Myth: "The person who prepared my tax return is liable for what's on there, not me. My accountant is on the hook for it."**

    Fact: You are liable for everything on your tax return. The tax preparer relies on you to furnish the facts, figures, miles, and numbers, but the taxpayer is still liable for any inaccuracies. Hiring a competent preparer can certainly prevent a lot of errors and omissions from making it onto your return in the first place, but if you give your accountant inflated expense figures and bloated mileage numbers, you're still on the hook for it. If the accountant makes a mistake, they should, and usually do, make it right with the client.

- **Myth: "If I file an extension, I'm much more likely to be audited."**
  Fact: This persistent rumor just isn't true. It's also not true that extended returns are less likely to be audited because the IRS is too busy auditing everyone who filed on time, that by the time you file your return in September or October that they won't have time for you. The IRS usually audits returns a year or two after the filing date anyway.

- **Myth: "The IRS cannot come into my house and inspect my home office, or even see if I have one."**
  Fact: By claiming a home office deduction, YOU are saying your home is a place of business. Should you get audited, the Internal Revenue Manual states that home offices should be examined, like any other business. You may not have to let them in, and it's unlikely they will refer it to the US Attorney and get a search warrant, but you will at the very least lose any deduction if you refuse to cooperate and likely be assessed with additional tax and penalties because your expenses will not be sustained.

IRS PAYMENT PLANS AND PROBLEM RESOLUTION

UNFILED TAX RETURNS

The IRS filed 447,000 liens in 2017, assessed $38 billion in civil penalties and initiated over one million investigations into unfiled tax returns the year before that. The IRS completed over 3,000 investigations and referred 2,200+ cases for criminal prosecution. Over 2,000 of those cases resulted in prison sentences.

The IRS does not play games, despite what some happy-go-lucky clients seem to think when they come into our office the first time with tax problems. If you haven't filed taxes for a number of years, it's a serious situation. <u>It's also a Federal felony that can get you more than a year in prison.</u>

Real estate agents and other self-employed individuals have a higher incidence of tax compliance problems than most of us who get a W2 and a regular paycheck with tax deductions taken out every two weeks.

It's much harder being an agent, working for maybe months between sales with nothing but a lot of talking to prospects, a lot of driving, and a lot of talk. Then maybe you earn a big commission check, and maybe you get nothing! No other profession is so solely dependent upon your ability to get the job done, and yet is so easily influenced by circumstances totally out of your control.

And it's not always possible to send the IRS 30% of that check when all is said and done. So an agent might have a banner year, make 50% more than they did the year before, and still not have the cash necessary to pay the taxes that will owe during the course of the year.

Sound familiar?

Some agents will take a crack at doing their own tax return on Turbo Tax, and be so frightened of the result that they never file it. And time goes on. They kind of try to forget about it, and hope they can get everything all filed and caught up before the IRS catches them. Next thing they know, four years have gone by.

Catching up on years of unfiled returns is a fairly common reason a new client comes to us. We need to address filing past-due returns first. If you have years of unfiled returns, get them filed. There is no sugarcoating this, and no getting around it.

Taxes for years where a return has not been filed cannot be discharged in bankruptcy, either.

Filing past due returns is the first, and most important, step in resolving your IRS case. Take your W2s, 1099s, business income and expenses, and whatever else, and pay a tax pro to prepare and file them. Or do it yourself, if you have skill to do so. If you have the records necessary to prepare your returns, you are halfway there already. Filing the returns stops the clock on the failure to file penalties, which can add up fast. The failure to file penalty is a penalty of 5% per month, failure to pay .05% per month, 1/10 the amount!

We run into a speed bump when the normal source documents

that tax preparers use to complete a return don't exist, or the client cannot find them. We have to get transcripts from the IRS or the state to figure out as best we can what income and withholding amounts the taxpayer had reported for them.

This can include information their broker filed with the IRS where we get their 1099s for commissions earned. We also will get everything filed by banks, mortgage companies, amounts for college expenses, health savings accounts, health insurance information, and other items. You can request account transcripts from the IRS that will detail all the wage and income that was reported to them by employers and other parties. If you haven't filed in a while, and aren't sure you have all your records, this is where you want to start!

You can call the IRS at 1-800-829-1040 and simply ask for your wage and income transcripts, or request copies online at IRS.gov.

These records contain a treasure trove of information about your tax case, and comprise much more information than most taxpayers realize. Authorized tax professionals can access all that same information on your behalf, too, if you're afraid of having to answer any uncomfortable IRS questions.

If you have a tax pro call the IRS, you don't have to be asked about where you bank, where you are employed, and your new address since they've last heard from you. If your new accountant doesn't have the answers to those intrusive questions at his fingertips, he can tell the IRS so, yet still get the information requested. You cannot!

From the transcripts you can determine what tax years you've not filed returns for, what the income items reported to the IRS were, and whether they filed a **Substitute for Return (SFR)** on you.

SUBSTITUTE FOR RETURN (SFR)

An SFR is filed when the taxpayer hasn't filed a tax return, so the IRS will take what information it has at hand, whether it be W2s from employers or any 1099 amounts from self-employment income and base a return solely from that information. Then they will bill you for the amount due. One of the many bad things about an SFR is that it does not consider any itemized deductions or business expenses you may have, nor will the IRS know about any business expenses for those that are self-employed.

So, a real estate agent may have a 1099 from her broker showing that she was paid $100,000 in commissions in a year. If our real estate agent doesn't file an income tax return, when the broker issues the 1099 like they are required to do by law, all the IRS knows is that she had $100,000 in income. The IRS won't know her expenses, which for most of our agent clients is usually 30% or more.

One problem created by SFRs is that while it is true that our agent had $80,000 in gross income (revenue) for her business, the IRS doesn't know she paid out $15,000 in website referral fees, paid an assistant, and had auto expenses, insurance, fuel, advertising, and office expense. And she is married with four children. Her real net income may have only been $15,000, and she gets much more benefit in the form of exemptions and married filing joint status than the IRS calculated on her SFR return.

What would have legitimately been maybe a $2,000 tax liability, with self-employment tax, is now over $40,000 based on the SFR that was filed. All because our hypothetical agent (who could be any number of clients we did actually help) didn't file her tax return. Maybe she had some charity deductions, and tax-deductible medical expenses that would add up to enough for her to owe nothing!

But the IRS doesn't know that since she didn't file a return. Now we have an individual who truly doesn't make a lot of money, facing a tax bill that exceeds her annual income! That is the reality of the situation we see in our tax practice every day.

State taxing agencies follow much the same protocol for filing SFRs, and the IRS has information sharing agreements with most states and many city taxing agencies. Talk about a disaster for non-filers. We have many new clients who have Federal, state and local SFR returns filed against them, and their debt with interest, penalties, fees, and collection costs can exceed 10 times the amount they would have really owed. Many taxpayers would end up homeless if they had to pay these amounts, even with an installment agreement over a number of years. Luckily, the IRS lets you file actual returns to replace the SFRs.

In our business, we always prepare State returns (for those with state income taxes) when engaged by a tax resolution client, because if there is an IRS problem, we know the State won't be far behind. Nobody dodges the IRS but still remembers and files their state all the taxes to which the state is entitled.

Depending upon the taxing district, we prepare the School District Income Tax and the city income tax returns as well (for tax-crazy states like Ohio). We had a recent client with 13 years of unfiled tax returns, and more IRS and State tax problems than will fit in this book.

The IRS filed SFRs for many of those years. The client had a giant box full of unopened W2s, 1099s, mortgage statements and other tax information going back 20 years. He and his wife would just throw everything in this box in the basement every year at tax time, and cross their fingers and hope the IRS would forget about them. When they wanted to sell their house and downsize into a condo since their children were grown and out of the house, they were surprised, to say the least, that the unfiled returns impeded their plans to quickly sell the long paid-off house and buy a luxury retirement condo in an upmarket suburban development.

After they hired our firm, we pulled their IRS transcripts and found they owed the IRS just under $200,000 with penalties and interest. We found numerous SFRs for various years; other years were unfiled with no SFR filed by the IRS.

What's really alarming is I saw that they had accuracy related penalties for sham deductions and fake dependents for one particular tax year. After about three hours on the phone with the IRS, while sending faxes back and forth at the same time, I was able to determine that this client was actually a victim of identity theft, in addition to being a chronic tax evader!

The couple's identities had been stolen and used to with a bogus $15,000 refund that was supposed to be direct deposited to a debit card in New York City. The only reason the phony

$15,000 refund wasn't initially sent, was that my clients had so many years of prior SFR and unfiled returns that the IRS took the bogus refund and applied it to their past due taxes!

Not long after the identity theft issue transpired, unbeknownst to my client (because they never opened any mail from the IRS), the IRS sent a notice asking them for verification for the deduction amounts that were used in the bogus return. They didn't open that letter either. Naturally, the IRS assumed that my clients had prepared the bogus return and sent it in themselves, in an attempt to defraud the U.S. Government.

When I got their case, the balance for that tax year alone was over $33,000 in taxes owed. After I got their supporting documentation and was able to prepare a proper return, and have the couple fill out Identity Theft Affidavits that were accepted by the IRS, they got a $700 refund. After filing all the required returns, we got this couple's nearly $200,000 balance down to $8,500, which they were easily able to pay from the proceeds from the sale of their house, and they were able to close on the sale of their house due to our work.

I included this story to show that no matter how bad you may think your tax situation is, <u>tax professionals see and resolve much worse cases than yours, every day.</u>

If you don't file your returns, you could have a substantial monetary penalty, you may not be able to discharge your tax debt in bankruptcy, and the IRS won't work out any form of payment plan, for any tax year, until those returns are filed. And there's that prison thing too.

The big turning point in getting yourself out of an IRS jam is to make the decision to get it taken care of now. When you make the decision you are going to get your tax problem resolved, it gets you in gear. You can round up what records you have, and take them to your local tax professional for help.

Start today!

Go to a tax pro who specializes in Tax Resolution – solving complex multi-year IRS issues is immensely more difficult than doing one year's tax return. We are members of the American Society of Tax Problem Solvers – a professional association of tax pros dealing with difficult tax problems.

Think of tax problems like a virulent disease: you don't just put your head in the sand and hope it goes away. You need to dig in and get treatment to solve the problem. Preparing past due returns or working out a financially painful payment plan can be emotionally raw and causes some clients substantial fear and anxiety.
By filing any past due tax returns, and staying current with filing returns, you prevent the problem from growing. You need to stop the clock on the penalties for Failure to File, as well as address any SFR issues as mentioned previously.

If you haven't filed your taxes yet for the current year and the deadline is coming, you have to either file or properly extend your return to get your old IRS problem resolved. Get your returns filed, even if you owe money that you don't have. You can work a payment plan out later, if you are in compliance with filing returns that are due.

DON'T PUT A BULLSEYE ON YOUR BACK

One item that will make a tax preparer think (know) a taxpayer is not giving him accurate numbers is when the client hands in a sheet and their mileage for the year is 20,000, their cell phone bill is $100 a month, their office expenses are $800, and their office and printing supplies are $1,000, and meals are $2,000. No! No, they weren't.

Your cell phone bill may be $105.67 a month with the federal taxes, and your office expenses may have been $778.41, and your printing and supplies were $1,041.25. You may have driven 19,847 miles. But let's just admit probably 0.00% of the self-employed people drive *exactly* 20,000 miles a year.

Use the right number!

> *NOTHING LOOKS MORE OBVIOUSLY FABRICATED THAN A TAX RETURN WITH COMPLETELY EVEN, WHOLE NUMBERS IN $100 INCREMENTS.*

Nothing looks more obviously fabricated than a tax return with completely even, whole numbers in $100 increments. You are signing your tax return, under penalty of perjury, that what you're sending the IRS is accurate!

A taxpayer who fills out a return like that will get completely torn apart in an audit, because the IRS agent will assume the taxpayer completely made up their numbers. And since the taxpayer did make up their numbers, they are not going to be able to go back and find receipts from the office store, the post office, the phone company, and the gas station to support the assertions made on the tax return down to the dollar. Estimates aren't good enough for a tax return. They don't count, not at all, despite the persistent and wishful rumors to the contrary. Taxpayers who make up expenses like that could easily find themselves facing civil fraud charges, substantial penalties, or much worse.

In the worst-case scenario, when records are unavailable, an accountant can invoke the *Cohan* rule*, which is a court case that allows taxpayers to deduct some of their business-related expenses even if the receipts have been lost or misplaced so long as they are reasonable and credible. The *Cohan* rule doesn't apply to mileage. We've used industry standard income and expense ratios from the IRS's own Market Segment Specialization Program (MSSP) data and analysis published by CCH and others.

IRS TAX DEBT RESOLUTION

Once you have your returns filed, most of the 'hard' work is done, and if you have IRS balances you still owe, there's several methods and procedures that you may be able to take advantage of, rather than just writing one big check to pay it all off at once.

You can, of course, write a check and pay the IRS all you owe at once, and for many taxpayers who have the cash flow and income to do this, it may make the most sense and be the most expeditious way to resolve your case. Paying your tax bill all at once, before the collections process begins, will prevent the IRS from hitting you with levies, liens, and garnishments.

> *You've probably seen the TV ads where a tax guy says he will settle your case for "Pennies on the Dollar."*

You've probably seen the TV ads where a tax guy says he will settle your case for "Pennies on the Dollar." We have clients every week who have heard these and other ads and believe that the IRS will wheel-and-deal and negotiate debts in every case. Some sales professionals like to believe that if you just present your case right, use a good close-the-deal strategy, do the ask-and-be-silent trick, and all the other best closing techniques that you can negotiate an IRS agent down just like the sales process employed in the selling of a house or a car.

IRS cases can be settled, but the pennies-on-the dollar tag

lines you hear are very deceiving. Those firms would take a big retainer over the phone on your credit card, and how they ended up going down in flames shows you how much faith to put in the 'pennies on the dollar' promise. The catchy ads with the pledge of erasing your debt because they knew some procedure that no one else did seemed too good to be true —because it was.

If you legitimately and rightfully owe the IRS, and you have the money and means to pay, you're chances of settling for a fraction of what you owe are very doubtful.

The most common categories of IRS payment/negotiation procedures are the following:

1. Installment Agreements (most common)
2. Currently Not Collectible
3. Penalty Abatement Request
4. Offers in Compromise

INSTALLMENT AGREEMENTS

If you owe under $50,000, its relatively easy to set up an installment agreement with the IRS. Payments are due in equal monthly payments, and generally you have up to 72 months to pay, as long as you are not under wage garnishment

or bank levy. If you owe over $25,000 and under $50,000, your payments must be directly debited from your bank account for individual taxes due.

Fill out a Form 9465 and send it to the IRS with this year's tax return, or you can call the IRS, or even set up a plan on the IRS.gov website.

Form **9465**
(Rev. January 2018)
Department of the Treasury
Internal Revenue Service

Installment Agreement Request

▶ Go to *www.irs.gov/Form9465* for instructions and the latest information.
▶ **If you are filing this form with your tax return, attach it to the front of the return.**
▶ See separate instructions.

OMB No. 1545-0074

Tip: If you owe $50,000 or less, you may be able to establish an installment agreement online, even if you have not yet received a bill for your taxes. Go to *www.irs.gov/opa* to apply for an Online Payment Agreement. See the instructions to find out when you are not required to file Form 9465.

Part I

This request is for Form(s) (for example, Form 1040 or Form 941) ▶
Enter tax year(s) or period(s) involved (for example, 2016 and 2017, or January 1, 2017 to June 30, 2017) ▶

1a Your first name and initial | Last name | Your social security number

If a joint return, spouse's first name and initial | Last name | Spouse's social security number

Current address (number and street). If you have a P.O. box and no home delivery, enter your box number. | Apt. number

City, town or post office, state, and ZIP code. If a foreign address, also complete the spaces below (see instructions).

Foreign country name | Foreign province/state/county | Foreign postal code

1b If this address is new since you filed your last tax return, check here . . . . ▶ ☐

2 Name of your business (must no longer be operating) | Employer identification number (EIN)

3 Your home phone number | Best time for us to call | **4** Your work phone number | Ext. | Best time for us to call

5 Enter the total amount you owe as shown on your tax return(s) (or notice(s)) . . . . . | **5**

6 If you have any additional balances due that aren't reported on line 5, enter the amount here (even if the amounts are included in an existing installment agreement) . . . . | **6**

7 Add lines 5 and 6 and enter the result . . . . | **7**

8 Enter the amount of any payment you are making with this request. See instructions . . . . | **8**

9 Amount owed. Subtract line 8 from line 7 and enter the result . . . . | **9**

10 Divide the amount on line 9 by 72 and enter the result . . . . | **10**

11a Enter the amount you can pay each month. Make your payment as large as possible to limit interest and penalty charges, **as these charges will continue to accrue until you pay in full**. If you have an existing installment agreement, this amount should represent your total proposed monthly payment amount for all your liabilities. **If no payment amount is listed on line 11a, a payment will be determined for you by dividing the balance due on line 9 by 72 months** . . . . . . | **11a** $

b If the amount on line 11a is less than the amount on line 10 and you are able to increase your payment to an amount that is equal to or greater than the amount on line 10, enter your *revised* monthly payment | **11b** $

• If you can't increase your payment on line 11b to more than or equal to the amount shown on line 10, check the box. Also, complete and attach Form 433-F, *Collection Information Statement* . . . . ☐

• If the amount on line 11a (or 11b, if applicable) is more than or equal to the amount on line 10 and the amount you owe is over $25,000 but not more than $50,000, then you do not have to complete Form 433-F. However, if you don't complete Form 433-F, then you must complete either line 13 or 14.

• If the amount on line 9 is greater than $50,000, complete and attach Form 433-F.

12 Enter the date you want to make your payment each month. **Don't** enter a date later than the 28th | **12**

13 If you want to make your payments by direct debit from your checking account, see the instructions and fill in lines 13a and 13b. This is the most convenient way to make your payments and it will ensure that they are made on time.

▶ **a** Routing number

▶ **b** Account number

I authorize the U.S. Treasury and its designated Financial Agent to initiate a monthly ACH debit (electronic withdrawal) entry to the financial institution account indicated for payments of my federal taxes owed, and the financial institution to debit the entry to this account. This authorization is to remain in full force and effect until I notify the U.S. Treasury Financial Agent to terminate the authorization. To revoke payment, I must contact the U.S. Treasury Financial Agent at **1-800-829-1040** no later than 14 business days prior to the payment (settlement) date. I also authorize the financial institutions involved in the processing of the electronic payments of taxes to receive confidential information necessary to answer inquiries and resolve issues related to the payments.

14 If you want to make your payments by payroll deduction, check this box and attach a completed Form 2159, *Payroll Deduction Agreement* . . . . ☐

Your signature | Date | Spouse's signature. If a joint return, both must sign. | Date

For Privacy Act and Paperwork Reduction Act Notice, see instructions. | Cat. No. 14842Y | Form **9465** (Rev. 1-2018)

If you owe over $50,000, things get a bit more complicated. You must complete a Form 433-A or 433-B, which is a complete financial disclosure. Everything you own, everything you earn, and everything you owe must be disclosed in detail. The IRS will figure out how much they think you can pay per month, and there is a little negotiation on allowable expenses, but not a lot.

The entire 433-A is six full pages long. I recommend that taxpayers do NOT represent themselves when doing this, it's kind of like someone who's not an attorney and knows nothing about the court system trying to <u>represent themselves in a murder trial!</u>

Form 433-A
(Rev. December 2012)
Department of the Treasury
Internal Revenue Service

Collection Information Statement for Wage Earners and Self-Employed Individuals

Wage Earners Complete Sections 1, 2, 3, 4, and 5 including the signature line on page 4. *Answer all questions or write N/A if the question is not applicable.*
Self-Employed Individuals Complete Sections 1, 3, 4, 5, 6 and 7 and the signature line on page 4. *Answer all questions or write N/A if the question is not applicable.*
For Additional Information, refer to Publication 1854, "How To Prepare a Collection Information Statement."
Include attachments if additional space is needed to respond completely to any question.

Name on Internal Revenue Service (IRS) Account	Social Security Number *SSN* on IRS Account	Employer Identification Number *EIN*

Section 1: Personal Information

1a Full Name of Taxpayer and Spouse *(if applicable)*	1c Home Phone ( )	1d Cell Phone ( )
1b Address *(Street, City, State, ZIP code) (County of Residence)*	1e Business Phone ( )	1f Business Cell Phone ( )
	2b Name, Age, and Relationship of dependent(s)	

2a Marital Status: ☐ Married ☐ Unmarried *(Single, Divorced, Widowed)*

	Social Security No. *(SSN)*	Date of Birth *(mmddyyyy)*	Driver's License Number and State
3a Taxpayer			
3b Spouse			

Section 2: Employment Information for Wage Earners

If you or your spouse have self-employment income instead of, or in addition to wage income, complete Business Information in Sections 6 and 7.

Taxpayer		Spouse	
4a Taxpayer's Employer Name		5a Spouse's Employer Name	
4b Address *(Street, City, State, and ZIP code)*		5b Address *(Street, City, State, and ZIP code)*	
4c Work Telephone Number ( )	4d Does employer allow contact at work ☐ Yes ☐ No	5c Work Telephone Number ( )	5d Does employer allow contact at work ☐ Yes ☐ No
4e How long with this employer *(years)* *(months)*	4f Occupation	5e How long with this employer *(years)* *(months)*	5f Occupation
4g Number of withholding allowances claimed on Form W-4	4h Pay Period: ☐ Weekly ☐ Bi-weekly ☐ Monthly ☐ Other	5g Number of withholding allowances claimed on Form W-4	5h Pay Period: ☐ Weekly ☐ Bi-weekly ☐ Monthly ☐ Other

Section 3: Other Financial Information *(Attach copies of applicable documentation)*

6	Are you a party to a lawsuit *(if yes, answer the following)*			☐ Yes	☐ No
	☐ Plaintiff ☐ Defendant	Location of Filing	Represented by	Docket/Case No.	
	Amount of Suit $	Possible Completion Date *(mmddyyyy)*	Subject of Suit		

7	Have you ever filed bankruptcy *(if yes, answer the following)*				☐ Yes	☐ No
	Date Filed *(mmddyyyy)*	Date Dismissed *(mmddyyyy)*	Date Discharged *(mmddyyyy)*	Petition No.	Location Filed	

8	In the past 10 years, have you lived outside of the U.S for 6 months or longer *(if yes, answer the following)*	☐ Yes	☐ No
	Dates lived abroad: from *(mmddyyyy)*	To *(mmddyyyy)*	

9a	Are you the beneficiary of a trust, estate, or life insurance policy *(if yes, answer the following)*		☐ Yes	☐ No
	Place where recorded:		EIN:	
	Name of the trust, estate, or policy	Anticipated amount to be received $	When will the amount be received	

9b	Are you a trustee, fiduciary, or contributor of a trust	☐ Yes	☐ No
	Name of the trust:	EIN:	

10	Do you have a safe deposit box (business or personal) *(if yes, answer the following)*		☐ Yes	☐ No
	Location *(Name, address and box number(s))*	Contents	Value $	

11	In the past 10 years, have you transferred any assets for less than their full value *(if yes, answer the following)*			☐ Yes	☐ No
	List Asset(s)	Value at Time of Transfer $	Date Transferred *(mmddyyyy)*	To Whom or Where was it Transferred	

www.irs.gov   Cat. No. 20312N   Form **433-A** (Rev.12-2012)

With any type of IRS installment agreement, each section must be filled out on the form, even if it doesn't apply to your case. Put N/A for not applicable or $0. The same rules apply for payment plans as they do for tax returns: round numbers in $100 increments don't fly for a whole page of numbers that are supposed to be to-the-dollar-accurate.

The 433-A in particular has areas for a detailed explanation of your monthly living expenses, including rent/mortgage, utilities, and food. Put the actual numbers in there! When you owe more than $50,000 you'll have to submit copies of your bank statements as well, and if the IRS agent reviewing your form sees that you claim $500 a month in utilities, and the bank statements show nothing of the sort, don't be surprised when your payment plan is rejected, and the IRS levies your bank account and garnishes your commissions.

If you have dependents that you support such as children or a dependent parent, here is where you can mention that and claim their dependent care expenses, necessary medical treatments, and other necessary and normal expenses.

> PRO-TIP: USE THE QUICK-SALE VALUE OF THE HOME, WHICH IS 80% OF THE FAIR MARKET VALUE, WHICH WILL LOWER THE DOLLAR AMOUNT ON THE 433-A TO LOWER YOUR REASONABLE COLLECTION POTENTIAL.

You'll have to list all your bank accounts, with account numbers and balances, and all your investments such as stocks, bonds, retirement accounts, and pensions.

All real estate must be detailed with address, any mortgage balance, and the current value.

Self-employed individuals such as real estate agents must disclose their monthly income and expenses or provide an annual profit & loss statement. Supporting bank statements are usually requested by the IRS for the business as well.

Business assets such as a company car, work computer, and other items must also be disclosed, and the IRS will allow reasonable business items to be used for business purposes. It's going to be better to list anything you use for business in the business section, rather than as personal, as you get an allowance for your business, so you can make money (So it's easier for you to pay the IRS.)

We had a client who owned a Rolls Royce automobile and had a nearly $1 million art collection, all of which we disclosed on their 433-A, and they were not forced to part with any of their prized possessions while they kept up their monthly payments on their $250,000 tax debt, so don't be afraid to the IRS will just willy-nilly seize your property. But plan on paying in full if you have sizeable assets or a large income.

You must also disclose any ownership interests you have in any corporations, partnerships or LLCs. Trusts should also be included. If the IRS believes you are not being truthful, your offer will be rejected. And like a tax return, an installment agreement request will require you to sign under the penalty of perjury.

OFFER IN COMPROMISE

An Offer in Compromise (OIC) is an agreement between a taxpayer and the Internal Revenue Service that allows the taxpayer to settle their tax debt for less than the full amount owed.

Individuals who have tax debts they can fully pay with an installment agreement or sale of assets don't qualify for an OIC in most cases. I want to stress, again: The IRS will not settle a tax case with an OIC if they believe the tax debt can be paid in full.

The IRS will use a Form 433-A OIC as a starting point to determine if the taxpayer has sufficient income and assets to pay their tax debt, and submit that with the Form 656 that is the actual Offer in Compromise form. The front page of Form 433-A OIC is on the next page.

Most Offers in Compromise that are accepted are for 'Doubt as to Collectability.' That simply means the IRS agrees that the taxpayer does not have the income potential or assets to pay their tax debt in full. The other two types of Offers are Doubt as to Liability, and Effective Tax Administration. Doubt as to Liability is as it sounds, that there is doubt or dispute as to whether you owe the amount, or the existence of the tax debt is correct under the law. Most of the time these are from the results of IRS examinations and the taxpayer has evidence that disputes all or some of the examination findings. Like with the Doubt as to Collectability OIC, the taxpayer makes them a dollar amount offer to settle the case.

Effective Tax Administration OICs are for cases where the taxpayer owes the amount in question, and could pay, but due to their exceptional circumstances it would be unjust to collect. A hypothetical example might be the case of an individual who earned a very high income, owed substantial back taxes, but then had a stroke and is now unable to work or care for himself. His money in the bank is sufficient to pay the IRS what he owes, but let's say the man's son administers that bank account and it's only sufficient to pay for home nursing care for the taxpayer, who is unable to work and will never be in a position to have that high income again. That's the type of circumstances the ETA OIC is for, and they are very rare.

It's important to tell clients working an Offer that they MUST stay current with the current year's estimated taxes (for self-employed individuals) or have the proper withholdings on W2s and investment income to stay in compliance. I had a client's failure (and refusal) to pay $7,500 in estimated taxes for a current tax year sink his OIC that would have saved him close to $100,000!

Stubbornness can have a price tag attached to it.

IRS COLLECTIONS

REASONABLE COLLECTION POTENTIAL

The IRS will come up with a number they call the Reasonable Collection Potential, if you want a minimum monthly payment plan on an amount over $50,000. Furthermore, the IRS won't accept an OIC unless the amount offered by a taxpayer is equal to or greater than the reasonable collection potential (RCP). The RCP is how the IRS measures the taxpayer's ability to pay, derived from taking the taxpayer's monthly income, and subtracting the allowable expenses that taxpayer has every month, in addition to the collection value of the taxpayer's assets. This is the summary of all the information on the 433-A.

The RCP includes the value that the IRS could get from the taxpayer's assets, such as the taxpayer's house, investment accounts, cars, bank accounts, and other property.

We had a client in Ohio with a $500,000 home, a $3,500 monthly mortgage, and a $90,000 car with a $1,500 monthly payment, and he and his wife were paying tuition for two kids in ivy league colleges. They were trying to work an Offer in Compromise. The clients came in and said, "We're broke!", and they said there was no way they could pay the IRS the $200,000+ they owed.

I had to tell them that it just wasn't going to fly with the IRS.

The IRS would say, "Yes you can pay!" Based on the clients

$20,000+ monthly income, they may have been able to afford to pay the mortgage on the 5-bedroom house on the golf course, the monthly payment on the Mercedes, eating at nice restaurants every day, and the other high-living items. They just couldn't afford ALL that stuff AND actually pay the taxes they owed. But they could have afforded to still live very well and paid their taxes.

> **THE RCP ALSO INCLUDES WHAT THE IRS WILL ESTIMATE YOUR FUTURE INCOME TO BE, AND THEY ALLOW FOR CERTAIN MINIMUM LIVING EXPENSES THAT THEY CALL IRS ALLOWABLE LIVING EXPENSES.**

I had to have a brutally honest discussion with the client to the effect: "Well, I guess if you spend everything you make, and wrack up a lot of debt on top of that, you're technically broke. That doesn't mean you cannot pay the IRS. It means you don't want to pay the IRS. What the IRS sees if you *won't*."

That's what Reasonable Collection Potential means, in human terms. In addition to property and other assets you own, the RCP also includes what the IRS will estimate your future income to be, and they allow for certain minimum living expenses that they call IRS Allowable Living Expenses.

And let's be honest, no one *really* wants to pay the IRS, but through ~~fear of prison~~, uh, excuse me, I meant through a sense of civic duty, almost all of us do pay our taxes.

The client in the example above made $200,000 - $300,000 a year as a real estate agent, and the IRS would evaluate not just his past income, but his future earning potential, as well, in coming up with the RCP number.

Collection Financial Standards are used to help determine what a taxpayer can reasonably pay on a payment plan for their past-due taxes. The Standards are the amounts that a taxpayer can spend per month on allowable expenses, and that amount of money will be exempt from the IRS collections process.

The IRS can allow you to spend more per month, before they collect your money, if they can be made to believe *the facts and circumstances of a taxpayer's situation indicate that using the standards is inadequate to provide for basic living expenses.*

I'd caution any taxpayer attempting to negotiate their own OIC to remember that the IRS employee on the other end of the phone is a government employee, and a human being. And that person has their own family, bills, and financial obligations. And they don't make a lot. They are likely going to be unsympathetic to claims that a vacation home, yacht, or country club membership is <u>a basic necessity,</u> and therefore you shouldn't have to pay your back taxes because you couldn't make the payment on your beach house if you actually paid your taxes! (A client wanted me to make almost that actual argument, and she was serious.)

You can make a one-time payment amount offer in your OIC, or pay it up to 24 months. Many clients cash in a retirement plan or borrow money from friends or family to fund their Offers.

The IRS calculates allowable living expenses for general categories, such as food, housekeeping, etc., and for each county in the country there is a corresponding housing amount that supposedly closely approximates the housing costs for each locality.

The table below represents the 'floor' or minimum expenses that the IRS will allow a taxpayer to earn each month and spend on necessary expenses to live on, before they will consider a tax debt collectible.

Based off the table below, for the 2018 tax year, the IRS will allow a taxpayer with the family of 4 to spend $3,676 each month on their total expenses before the amount above that is considered collectible, based on a location of Columbus, Ohio. The IRS website has a listing for each county in the country. So if the taxpayer in the example below made $4,500 per month, the amount of Reasonable Collection Potential would be $824 a month.

2019 Allowable Living Expenses National Standards

Expense	One Person	Two Persons	Three Persons	Four Persons
Food	$386	$685	$786	$958
Housekeeping supplies	$40	$72	$76	$76
Apparel & services	$88	$159	$169	$243
Personal care products & services	$43	$70	$76	$91
Miscellaneous	$170	$302	$339	$418
Total	$727	$1,288	$1,446	$1,786

More than four persons	Additional Persons Amount
For each additional person, add to four-person total allowance:	$420

Housing -- Franklin County, Ohio	$ 1,437.00	$ 1,687.00	$ 1,778.00	$ 1,982.00
Total Allowable Living Monthly Expenses	$ 2,164.00	$ 2,975.00	$ 3,224.00	$ 3,768.00

The taxpayer would not be compelled by the IRS to pay more than $824 a month, even if they owed $500,000 to the IRS. The bad news for those with tax debts they don't want to pay is that the IRS will use levies, liens and garnishments – even the forced sale of your home -- to get what you owe if you won't agree 'voluntarily' to pay.

The good news is the IRS will at least allow taxpayers to have the minimum expenses to live on each month, and collect that amount above what the IRS doesn't consider a taxpayer 'needs.'

Other extenuating circumstances include necessary medical expenses, which the IRS can add back to the minimum expenses if necessary. We have a client that owed the IRS over $100,000, and the married couple made over $100,000 per year. Under normal circumstances, they could have paid the IRS and lived just fine. They might not have thought so, but they wouldn't have starved and would have kept their house.

But they also had twin boys with autism, who required very expensive and exhaustive specialized treatment at a special school every day. The cost of this treatment was over $2,500 a month, and after we were able to prove the validity, necessity, and existence of this treatment expense we were able to add this additional amount to their allowable living expenses.

THE COLLECTION STATUTE EXPIRATION DATE (CSED)

The Collection Statute Expiration Date is the statute of limitations on how long the IRS has to collect a tax debt. Generally, there is a ten-year statute of limitations on IRS collections for income taxes. This means that the IRS can attempt to collect your unpaid taxes for up to ten years from the date they were assessed, <u>not</u> when the tax was originally due or when the return was filed. If a taxpayer's 2014 1040 return was filed on April 1, 2015, and the IRS assesses a taxpayer $1,000 (meaning that's the day they officially say you owe the money) on February 1, 2016 for a forgotten 1099 amount for the 2015 tax year, the assessment date will run from February 1, 2016 for 10 years.

Generally, the IRS has to stop its collection efforts after that 10 years is up, but there are some important exceptions.

Those exceptions that stop the clock on the CSED include filing an Offer in Compromise, filing for bankruptcy, filing a lawsuit against the IRS and some other items. Each of those items essentially extend the statute of limitations on the amount of time the IRS has to collect on a tax case.

Liens filed on a property for income tax are self-released after the ten years expire. It may make sense for taxpayers that have several years of past due taxes due <u>that aren't currently in collections</u> to put it off until a year that is just about to expire 'falls off' the calendar, and then negotiate on just the remaining tax year's liabilities.

For instance, if a taxpayer has set up facts as in the table below:

If filed prior to CSED on 2005 Tax Year	
Past Tax Year	Amount Owed
2005	$ 10,000
2006	$ 12,000
2009	$ 5,000
2010	$ 7,500
	$34,500

If filed after CSED date for 2005 Tax Year	
Past Tax Year	Amount Owed
2006	$ 12,000
2009	$ 5,000
2010	$ 7,500
	$24,500

Let's say the $10,000 due for 2005 expires on July 1 of this year. It wouldn't make a lot of sense for the taxpayer to negotiate a payment plan on the full $34,500 in tax debt in May of this year, if they could get away with waiting 2 months for the $10,000 from the tax year 2005 to expire. Sometimes you can stretch out the clock, but sometimes not, it depends on the facts and circumstances of your case.

That's why it's important to get a complete IRS transcript investigation done and make sure the CSED dates are calculated properly. If you've had IRS problems for a number of years, it may save you a lot of money!

IRS LIENS

If a taxpayer owes the IRS money, the IRS can file a lien at the County Recorder, County Clerk or other real estate office where the taxpayer lives to secure the government's interest in taxpayer's property when they don't pay their tax debt. Tax liens filed on income taxes are self-releasing after 10 years.

What the lien says on its face does not necessarily mean that is what the current IRS balance is. Payments, credits, the processing of newly filed or amended returns all effect the IRS balance being paid in full.

The IRS doesn't need to be paid the face amount of the lien for it to be released, and it can be released without the total IRS balance being paid in full.

A lien may be released early if the taxpayer, or their representative, files a Form 12277 with the IRS, and something can be worked out. I've worked out cases where a lien was released with a partial payment of the taxes paid, and the client agreed to set up an installment agreement where the remainder was paid off over 14 months with direct debits from their checking account.

LIEN SUBORDINATION

A lien can also be 'subordinated', which means you can get a property refinanced without having to fully pay off the IRS. IRS Form 14134 on the next page. If you need to refinance a property, but are not able to pay the tax in full, the IRS may agree to subordinate the IRS lien 'behind' a new mortgage. This subordination of the IRS lien makes the lender's security interest superior or prior to the tax lien (in "first position").

The lien remains in place and continues to encumber the property, so you cannot sell it outright. The subordination could be in the IRS's best interest because the IRS receives funds from the refinancing (maybe you do a cash-out refinance and give them $10,000 at close), or the interest rate is low enough that you can pay them larger monthly installments.

To apply for the subordination, you need a draft closing document, and pretty much all the items you'd need for a closing, as well:

- Legal description of the property.
- A copy of the loan agreement
- A copy of the tax lien.
- Information regarding the priority lien holder
- A draft closing statement with all costs and proceeds of funds
- Two appraisals of the property
- The closing date and location for the sale of the property

To apply for a certificate of lien subordination, see IRS Publication 784, How to Prepare an Application for a Certificate of Subordination of a Federal Tax Lien, a copy of which is on page 197 and on your CD.

Form **14134** (June 2010)

Department of the Treasury — Internal Revenue Service

Application for Certificate of Subordination of Federal Tax Lien

OMB No. 1545-2174

Complete the entire application. Enter NA (not applicable), when appropriate. Attachments and exhibits should be included as necessary. Additional information may be requested to clarify the details of the transaction(s).

1. Taxpayer Information (Individual or Business named on the notice of lien)

Name (Individual First, Middle Initial, Last) or (Business) as it appears on lien	Primary Social Security Number (last 4 digits only)
Name Continuation (Individual First, Middle Initial, Last) or (Business) d/b/a	Secondary Social Security Number (last 4 digits only)
Address (Number, Street, P.O. Box)	Employer Identification Number

City	State	ZIP Code

Telephone Number (with area code)	Fax Number (with area code)

2. Applicant Information ☐ Check if also the Taxpayer (If not the taxpayer, attach copy of lien. See Sec.10)

Name (First, Middle Initial, Last)	Relationship to taxpayer

Address (Number, Street, P.O. Box)

City	State	ZIP Code

Telephone Number (with area code)	Fax Number (with area code)

3. Property Owner ☐ Check if also the Applicant

Relationship to Taxpayer

4. Attorney/Representative Information — Attached: Form 8821 or Power of Attorney Form 2848 ☐ Yes ☐ No

Name (First, Middle Initial, Last)	Interest Represented (e.g. taxpayer, lender, etc.)

Address (Number, Street, P.O. Box)

City	State	ZIP Code

Telephone Number (with area code)	Fax Number (with area code)

5. Lending/Finance Company

Company Name	Contact Name	Contact Phone Number

Type of transaction (For example, loan consolidation, refinance, etc)

Catalog Number 54726H   www.irs.gov   Form **14134** (Rev. 06-2010)

LEVIES

An IRS levy actually takes your property, like your house or a financial account, to pay the tax debt. If a delinquent taxpayer does not enter into an agreement to 'voluntarily' pay their tax debt, the IRS can levy, seize and sell any type of real or personal property that you own or have an interest in. The IRS can, and frequently does, levy bank accounts. We have numerous clients come to us to help them with their tax problems only after they've had their bank account wiped out by the IRS.

Some of these clients had been getting IRS notices for years and thought that nothing would ever happen. But now their checking account balance is $0, the rent is due, the car payment is late, and they wish they'd come to our office months ago!

When you get a levy notice, you really need to act quickly to avoid having your property seized. Very often in these cases when they say respond in 30 days, they really mean it.

GARNISHMENTS / WAGE LEVIES

The IRS can also garnish your wages if you are an employee, or your commission payments due you if are a 1099 independent contractor. The IRS calls it wage levy, but it's all the same thing to you. It's embarrassing for real estate agents or insurance agents to have their broker deal with the hassle of taking half the commission for each sale and send it to the IRS instead of you. This can be avoided by entering into an installment agreement.

TAXES AND YOUR CLIENTS

PRIMARY RESIDENCE CAPITAL GAINS TAX EXCLUSION

One of the biggest tax misunderstandings regarding real estate is the matter of capital gains on a primary residence. The IRS regards the primary residence as the place where a taxpayer lives. Section 121 of The Internal Revenue Code states that taxpayers who have lived in the home for at least two of the previous five tax years prior to the date of the sale can exclude up to $250,000 in profit from capital gains taxes ($500,000 for married filed joint.) Improvements that are of a permanent nature are added to the basis of the property.

For example, a married couple filing jointly has the following details regarding the sale of their house:

Example:

Jan 1, 2005 purchased house for	$200,000
June 15, 2015 homeowner paid renovations	$ 75,000
Total basis:	$275,000
October 2, 2018 sold house for	$750,000
Total gain: ($750,000 - $275,000)	$475,000
Total taxable gain:	$ 0

This Section 121 exclusion has two basic criteria, ownership and use. You must own the home for two out of the five preceding years, and use it as your primary residence.

Taxpayers are generally not eligible for the exclusion if they've taken the exclusion on another home in the last two years.

Most real estate transactions with proceeds over $250,000 generate a 1099-S *Proceeds from Real Estate Transactions,* so you will still report the sale on such a house on your 1040, but will not owe tax if you meet the criteria above.

One item to consider is the recapture of any depreciation for home office expense that were taken (another reason why we recommend not depreciating your home for home office). This tax break does not count for rental homes or vacation homes, just the taxpayer's primary residence.

WHAT A GREAT TAX BREAK!

Short or temporary absences are still counted as periods of use, even if you rent the property out when you are gone. For example, if a client went to Europe for three months and rented their house out in their absence, that three months would still count toward the two years and not be held against them.

Reduced Exclusions
A taxpayer who owned and used a home for less than two years would not normally meet the ownership and use test, may have a reduced capital gains tax exclusion in some cases. This may pertain if the house was sold due to unforeseen circumstances.

Unforeseen circumstances are situations such as:
- Involuntary conversion of the property (such as loss to eminent domain)
- Damage from a natural disaster or act of war

- Unemployment – loss of your or a spouse's job
- Change of job that requires a move of at least 50 miles in distance greater than the distance from the location of the old home to the old place of employment
- Multiple births from the same pregnancy
- Other extraordinary circumstances that the IRS has discretion to consider

To figure the reduced deduction, you take the amount of the exclusion ($250,000 single/$500,000 joint) and multiply by the number of days or months that apply.

Let's say a couple sells their house after 16 months, and had to do so because of the loss of a job and the birth of quadruplets. They bought the house for $500,000 16 months ago, and sold it for $900,000 today. They meet neither the time nor use test, but qualify for a reduced exclusion.

Example

Jan 1, 2017 purchase price	$500,000
April 30, 2018 sale price	$900,000
Gross capital gain:	$400,000
% of Reduction (16/24) months =	2/3 excluded
2/3 x $400,000 excluded =	$266,666.67
Taxable amount of gain ($400,000 - $266,666.67) =	$133,333.33

With our fast-moving economy and the frequency of people moving for work reasons, this is a valuable bit of knowledge for a real estate agent to have, as most real estate agents don't know these rules.

It could very well get you some listings and sales you might not otherwise have gotten!

1031 LIKE-KIND EXCHANGES

All real estate agents need to have some working knowledge of how like-kind exchanges work. Many investors and owners of rental properties are always on the prowl for the opportunity to exchange business or investment properties. Under a 1031 exchange, the taxpayer does not have a taxable gain and doesn't deduct any losses until the property the buyer just received is eventually sold.

A like-kind exchange is a transaction, or a series of transactions, that allows the owner of one or more properties to dispose of a property and replace it with another asset without incurring any taxes from the sale of the first property.

The exchange must be for like-kind property, such as real estate for real estate, or personal property for personal property. The exchange of farmland for rental building would qualify for like-kind, since both are real estate. An outright sale of a property for cash does not qualify.

- The property must be held for business use, such as a rental or business building. Your personal residence does not count
- The property must not be primarily for sale – such as inventory or new home sales
- There must be an exchange of two or more properties
- For a deferred exchange, the property received must be identified within 45 days after the date of transfer of the property given up
- The replacement property must be received by the 180th day after the date the property that was given up was transferred

- Or the due date, including extensions, of the tax return for the year in which the transfer happens
- Like-kind exchanges are reported on IRS form 8824

You'll see that the form 8824, which will be filed with your tax return, calls for the following information:

- The descriptions of the properties exchanged
- The dates that properties were identified and transferred
- Any relationship between the parties to the exchange
- Value of the like-kind and other property received (boot)
- Gain or loss on sale of other (non-like-kind) property given up
- Cash received or paid; liabilities relieved or assumed
- Adjusted basis of like-kind property given up; and any realized gain

A properly executed 1031 exchange requires a Qualified Intermediary to be used to facilitate the transaction. These individuals are also sometimes called Exchange Accommodators or 1031 Exchange Facilitators. The funny thing is that although the law calls for a Qualified Intermediary to be used, they are generally not licensed or regulated in any way.

Below is a warning from the IRS that I think is so particularly well-written on 1031 exchanges I include it verbatim:

From the IRS:
> *"You should note, and advise your clients, it's important to know that taking the cash or other proceeds before the exchange is complete may disqualify the entire transaction from like-kind exchange treatment and make ALL gain immediately taxable.*
>
> *If cash or other proceeds that are not like-kind property are received at the conclusion of the exchange, the transaction will still qualify as a like-kind exchange. Gain may be taxable, but only to the extent of the proceeds that are not like-kind property.*
>
> *One way to avoid premature receipt of cash or other proceeds is to use a qualified intermediary or other exchange facilitator to hold those proceeds until the exchange is complete.*

> *You cannot act as your own facilitator. In addition, your agent (including your real estate agent or broker, investment banker or broker, accountant, attorney, employee or*

anyone who has worked for you in those capacities within the previous two years) cannot act as your facilitator.

Be careful in your selection of a qualified intermediary as there have been recent incidents of intermediaries declaring bankruptcy or otherwise being unable to meet their contractual obligations to the taxpayer. These situations have resulted in taxpayers not meeting the strict timelines set for a deferred or reverse exchange, thereby disqualifying the transaction from Section 1031 deferral of gain. The gain may be taxable in the current year while any losses the taxpayer suffered would be considered under separate code sections." IRS FS-2008-18, February 2008.

SECTION 1033 INVOLUNTARY CONVERSIONS

Real estate agents near flood zones or tornado areas pay attention! An involuntary conversion is when the owner's property is lost, destroyed or damaged and the property owner gets paid by the government (for right of way, seizure through eminent domain etc.), or insurance company or some other form of payment.

Under 1033, a property owner can elect to defer reporting gain on an involuntary conversion if they receive insurance or disaster relief money and invest it into another property that is similar to the one they lost. This doesn't apply to personal use property, except in the case of theft or what is called a casualty loss.

For cases such as when a hurricane destroys a rental property, gain or loss from the conversion is usually claimed on the tax return during the year in which the loss or the gain occurs. The owner can choose to delay reporting the gain under section 1033, for up to three years for residential rentals and office buildings.

If a property owner had a $400,000 basis in his rental duplex that was destroyed by a tornado, and he received a settlement of $500,000, that sounds like a $100,000 gain, does it not? But under 1033, the taxpayer has up to three years later to invest those funds in a replacement property. If he were to invest less than $500,000 in a replacement property, the amount of that cash he kept or otherwise spent would be considered gain.

Condemned property follows much the same rules.

RENTAL INCOME AND EXPENSES

Rental properties are probably the most popular form of investment property in the United States. Owning rentals is popular because it allows the landlord to own a property, and have the tenant's monthly rent pay substantially all the bills for the purchase, maintenance and upkeep up the property.

If a property owner owns the property outright, with no mortgage, the owner can make decent income on a monthly basis. Even with a mortgage, savvy landlords can still turn a profit and have the tenants pay all the bills, so that the landlord owns the property and the tenants pay off the mortgage for them over time. The goal being the rental property is paid off from cash flow generated by from the renter, with as little as possible coming from the landlord.

I get rental properties, and have had the landlord blues for a long time. After the crash of 2007-2008, I was stuck with a rental house that was dramatically underwater, and a crazy cat lady hoarder was the tenant who I could not get rid of until it was too late.

Besides having my own rental properties, I've been involved in numerous partnerships in rentals as well. It's not a coincidence that we do a lot of accounting and tax work for landlords.

Rental properties have their own little universe of rules, and real estate agents need to know them, because your clients will have questions and its helpful to know the rules and the language that investors speak and deal in.

The landlord claims the rental income on their tax return, and deducts the allowable expenses. Individuals report rentals on Schedule E of their tax return, and companies report rental activities on Form 8825 on the S Corp or Partnership return.

The income part is easy, the owner for the property just reports the amount of income earned. Expenses and how to properly account for them financially on a tax return is what confuses a lot of property owners.

A taxpayer (other than a real estate professional) cannot deduct the loss from any vacant rental property – a property must be available for rent to claim expenses.

Depreciation is the reduction of value of an asset, over the passage of time. For tax purposes, this means that for a residential rental house the owner deprecates the cost of the property over the useful life of the property, which is 27.5 years. For commercial property, this is 39 years.

Depreciation vs. Expense works like this: if we were depreciating a $100 item over 5 years, it would be $20 a year for the next 5 years. If we were expensing an item, it would be $100 this year.

In plain English, if you buy a rental house for $100,0000, you can claim $3,636.36 per year over the next 27.5 years as your depreciation expense. About half our landlord clients want to argue with us about this, but you do not get to write off your whole monthly mortgage payment on your taxes. Just the interest.

The principal is being written off in the form of depreciation, if you want to look at it that way.

The great Repairs vs. Improvements debate is another contentious issue regarding rentals, and taxpayers naturally want to write off as much as they can every year to minimize their taxable income. Repairs are expenses to keep a property in working order, things such as fixing broken light switches and replacing worn-out doorknobs.

Improvements are items that add to the value of the property or increase its useful life and must be depreciated. A new roof, a remodeled kitchen, a new bathroom, or all new flooring would all be examples of improvements that must be depreciated. The IRS is very specific about what constitutes a repair as opposed to an improvement.

We've seen many landlords be audited, and all repair and improvement receipts and documentation are always requested right at the beginning of the audit by IRS agent, so be cautious.

Common rental expenses:
- Mortgage interest
- Property taxes
- Depreciation
- Repairs
- Insurance
- Advertising
- Home office (if qualified)
- Maintenance
- Improvements
- Inspection fees
- Utilities

- Cleaning
- Credit check and background screening
- Mowing
- Property management fees
- Accounting and legal fees
- Supplies
- Mileage related to management of the property

There are some special rules regarding rental properties, since the IRS considers the ownership of rental properties to be a passive activity. This means, under many circumstances, rental losses may not be used to offset active income. Landlords may be able to deduct up to $25,000 in losses for rentals in which they actively participate, if their modified adjusted gross income is under $100,000, and is phased out for those making more than $150,000. This $25,000 rule does not apply to estate professionals. Real estate professionals can take 100% of their losses.

There are some special rules and related tax advantages to those engaged in rental real estate as a business, rather than an investment. Real estate agents are already real estate professionals and can take advantage of these special breaks.

When your activity rises to the level of a business, you continue to report the rentals on Schedule E, but with the business classification, you qualify for:

- Tax-favored Section 1231 treatment;
- Business use of an office in your home;
- Business (versus investment) treatment of meetings, seminars, and conventions; and
- Section 179 treatment of your business-use assets. 179 expensing lets you write off a taxpayer to deduct the cost of assets in one year, rather than over multiple years. (i.e.: You can write off a $1,000 computer now, rather than take $200 for the next 5 years, for instance).

Form **8825** (Rev. November 2018) Department of the Treasury Internal Revenue Service

Rental Real Estate Income and Expenses of a Partnership or an S Corporation

► Attach to Form 1065 or Form 1120S.
► Go to www.irs.gov/Form8825 for the latest information.

OMB No. 1545-0123

Name | Employer identification number

1 Show the type and address of each property. For each rental real estate property listed, report the number of days rented at fair rental value and days with personal use. See instructions. See page 2 to list additional properties.

	Physical address of each property—street, city, state, ZIP code	Type—Enter code 1-8; see page 2 for list	Fair Rental Days	Personal Use Days
A				
B				
C				
D				

		Properties A	Properties B	Properties C	Properties D
Rental Real Estate Income					
2 Gross rents	2				
Rental Real Estate Expenses					
3 Advertising	3				
4 Auto and travel	4				
5 Cleaning and maintenance	5				
6 Commissions	6				
7 Insurance	7				
8 Legal and other professional fees	8				
9 Interest (see instructions)	9				
10 Repairs	10				
11 Taxes	11				
12 Utilities	12				
13 Wages and salaries	13				
14 Depreciation (see instructions)	14				
15 Other (list) ►	15				
16 Total expenses for each property. Add lines 3 through 15	16				
17 Income or (loss) from each property. Subtract line 16 from line 2	17				

18a Total gross rents. Add gross rents from line 2, columns A through H	18a	
b Total expenses. Add total expenses from line 16, columns A through H	18b	( )
19 Net gain (loss) from Form 4797, Part II, line 17, from the disposition of property from rental real estate activities	19	
20a Net income (loss) from rental real estate activities from partnerships, estates, and trusts in which this partnership or S corporation is a partner or beneficiary (from Schedule K-1)	20a	
b Identify below the partnerships, estates, or trusts from which net income (loss) is shown on line 20a. Attach a schedule if more space is needed.		
(1) Name / (2) Employer identification number		
21 Net rental real estate income (loss). Combine lines 18a through 20a. Enter the result here and on: • Form 1065 or 1120S: Schedule K, line 2	21	

For Paperwork Reduction Act Notice, see instructions. Cat. No. 10136Z Form **8825** (Rev. 11-2018)

Form 8825 Rentals for S Corps

RENTALS AS A BUSINESS

As we've said, rental real estate is usually considered a passive activity, and generally taxpayers want it to be an active activity instead. In the Levy case, the tax court ruled that the trustees of this estate, by renting the real estate, were engaged in a trade or business. The court then went on to say this:

"Courts have consistently held that the rental of real estate is a "trade or business" if the taxpayer-lessor engages in regular and continuous activity in relation to the property. It has been held that a taxpayer who rents only a single parcel of real estate is engaged in the "trade or business" of renting real estate if his activities are regular and continuous. The fact that the trustees employed agents to manage the real property does not make any difference."

So, if your rentals rise to the level of being a "Trade or Business", it opens the door for you to write off more expenses, such as home office, and take more losses in a current year.

SECTION 1231

Section 1231 property refers to real or depreciable business property held for over a year. Section 1231 property includes buildings, machinery, land and a slew of other things unrelated to real estate. When you hear about 1231 gains, this is what people are talking about. We are talking about rental and other properties here, specifically.

The two big tax benefits of Section 1231 treatment are:

- You can net Section 1231 losses as ordinary losses that you use to offset ordinary income – like real estate commissions
- Section 1231 gains are long-term capital gains, so they are generally taxed at a lower rate than other income

This gives you the best of both worlds: ordinary losses and long-term capital gains.

HOME OFFICE EXPENSES FOR RENTAL PROPERTIES

If your rental business rises to the level of a <u>trade or business</u>, you can deduction home office expenses for it. In Curphy vs. Commissioner, the Tax Court ruled that the petitioner's ownership and management from his home of three condo units, two townhouses, and one single-family home rose to the level of a trade or business for purposes of his claiming the home-office deduction. That deduction would not have been allowed had he just been a real estate investor, the distinction is that he was engaged in a <u>trade or business</u>. The requirement that the office be used regularly and exclusively still applies, though.

MEETINGS, SEMINARS, AND CONVENTIONS

There is no allowable deduction for travel or other costs of attending a convention, seminar, or similar meeting unless the activity relates to a trade or business of the taxpayer.

We had clients who attended a $15,000, heavily advertised, real estate seminar and they had only one rental house that they really didn't actively manage. Both husband and wife were physicians and truly passive owners. Thus, if your rental property is an investment, like my doctors, kiss those deductions goodbye for rental property conventions, seminars, and similar meetings. $15,000 is a lot to pay for something you cannot write off!

SECTION 179 EXPENSING

With respect to rental properties and Section 179 expensing, you need to pay attention to the following two rules, which can impact your expensing:

- You may not claim Section 179 expensing on most assets used for residential rental properties.
- To qualify for Section 179 expensing, you must purchase and place the property in use in the active conduct of your business. (179 is expensing items, rather than depreciating assets over time, and lowers your current year taxable liability. You may be able to 179 Expense a $1,000 this year on your taxes, instead of taking $200 for each of the next five years, for instance.)

SALE OF RENTAL PROPERTIES

When a property owner sells a rental property, they must recapture their past depreciation on their income tax return during the year of the sale. If a client had a rental property they bought for $150,000, and they had depreciated $50,000 of it, and sold the property for $200,000, for instance, their gain would be $100,000.

This would be the perfect time to advise your client about the possibility of a like-kind exchange. (You can get a commission on the sale, and convince them to buy another property for the tax-free exchange – **thereby earning two commissions** – and saving your client money at the same time!)

Sales of business property, like rentals, is reported on Form 4797.

The 4797 on the below shows how the taxable gain is calculated on a rental property.

Form 4797

Sales of Business Property
(Also Involuntary Conversions and Recapture Amounts Under Sections 179 and 280F(b)(2))

▶ Attach to your tax return.
▶ Go to www.irs.gov/Form4797 for instructions and the latest information.

OMB No. 1545-0184

2018

Department of the Treasury
Internal Revenue Service

Attachment Sequence No. 27

Name(s) shown on return | Identifying number

1 Enter the gross proceeds from sales or exchanges reported to you for 2018 on Form(s) 1099-B or 1099-S (or substitute statement) that you are including on line 2, 10, or 20. See instructions . . . . | 1 |

Part I — Sales or Exchanges of Property Used in a Trade or Business and Involuntary Conversions From Other Than Casualty or Theft—Most Property Held More Than 1 Year (see instructions)

2 (a) Description of property	(b) Date acquired (mo., day, yr.)	(c) Date sold (mo., day, yr.)	(d) Gross sales price	(e) Depreciation allowed or allowable since acquisition	(f) Cost or other basis, plus improvements and expense of sale	(g) Gain or (loss) Subtract (f) from the sum of (d) and (e)

3 Gain, if any, from Form 4684, line 39 . . . . | 3 |
4 Section 1231 gain from installment sales from Form 6252, line 26 or 37 . . . . | 4 |
5 Section 1231 gain or (loss) from like-kind exchanges from Form 8824 . . . . | 5 |
6 Gain, if any, from line 32, from other than casualty or theft . . . . | 6 |
7 Combine lines 2 through 6. Enter the gain or (loss) here and on the appropriate line as follows . . . | 7 |

Partnerships and S corporations. Report the gain or (loss) following the instructions for Form 1065, Schedule K, line 10, or Form 1120S, Schedule K, line 9. Skip lines 8, 9, 11, and 12 below.

Individuals, partners, S corporation shareholders, and all others. If line 7 is zero or a loss, enter the amount from line 7 on line 11 below and skip lines 8 and 9. If line 7 is a gain and you didn't have any prior year section 1231 losses, or they were recaptured in an earlier year, enter the gain from line 7 as a long-term capital gain on the Schedule D filed with your return and skip lines 8, 9, 11, and 12 below.

8 Nonrecaptured net section 1231 losses from prior years. See instructions . . . . | 8 |
9 Subtract line 8 from line 7. If zero or less, enter -0-. If line 9 is zero, enter the gain from line 7 on line 12 below. If line 9 is more than zero, enter the amount from line 8 on line 12 below and enter the gain from line 9 as a long-term capital gain on the Schedule D filed with your return. See instructions . . . . | 9 |

Part II — Ordinary Gains and Losses (see instructions)

10 Ordinary gains and losses not included on lines 11 through 16 (include property held 1 year or less):

11 Loss, if any, from line 7 . . . . | 11 (|) |
12 Gain, if any, from line 7 or amount from line 8, if applicable . . . . | 12 |
13 Gain, if any, from line 31 . . . . | 13 |
14 Net gain or (loss) from Form 4684, lines 31 and 38a . . . . | 14 |
15 Ordinary gain from installment sales from Form 6252, line 25 or 36 . . . . | 15 |
16 Ordinary gain or (loss) from like-kind exchanges from Form 8824 . . . . | 16 |
17 Combine lines 10 through 16 . . . . | 17 |
18 For all except individual returns, enter the amount from line 17 on the appropriate line of your return and skip lines a and b below. For individual returns, complete lines a and b below.

  a If the loss on line 11 includes a loss from Form 4684, line 35, column (b)(ii), enter that part of the loss here. Enter the loss from income-producing property on Schedule A (Form 1040), line 16. (Do not include any loss on property used as an employee.) Identify as from "Form 4797, line 18a." See instructions . . . . | 18a |
  b Redetermine the gain or (loss) on line 17 excluding the loss, if any, on line 18a. Enter here and on Schedule 1 (Form 1040), line 14 | 18b |

For Paperwork Reduction Act Notice, see separate instructions.   Cat. No. 13086I   Form **4797** (2018)

INSTALLMENT SALES

Installment sales are when a property sells, and at least one payment is expected to be received after the tax year in which the sale occurs. The property owner may sell the property and receive payments over multiple years, and can use the installment method of reporting that sale to report a portion of the gain over multiple years, perhaps keeping that property owner in a lower tax bracket.

The property owner's gain, which is basically their profit, is the amount the sales price exceeds their basis. If a seller is selling a property directly to a buyer, with no mortgage, it would look like:

$$\text{The profit percentage} = \frac{\text{Profit} \quad \$15{,}000}{\text{Sale Price} \quad \$100{,}000}$$

$$\text{Profit percentage} = 15\%$$

To calculate the profit for each year in an installment sale, simply take the 15% and multiply that by the payment amount received from the buyer. If the seller receives $20,000 a year for the next 5 years, $3,000 would be profit (15% x $20,000).

Installment Sale Gross Profits	Income	Expense
Selling Price of property	100	
Ajdusted basis of propety		50
Selling Expenses		25
Any depreciation recapture		10
add the expenses		85
Subtract expense from income		15
Divide line above by selling price		15%
this is your Gross Profit %		15%

Profit percentage = 15%

REAL ESTATE AGENT S CORP ISSUES IN OHIO

We've had some issues in our practice where the broker refuses to pay the agent's commissions to their S Corp, citing some vague rule of the Ohio Division of Real Estate or the Ohio Revised Code. To make things simple for you, if you set up an S Corp and you sell Real Estate in Ohio, we've put the law below that specifically allows for Agent's commissions to be paid directly to their S Corp or LLC:

> ***Ohio Revised Code 4735.20 Commissions, fees, or other compensation.***
>
> *(C) A licensed real estate broker may pay all or part of a fee, commission, or other compensation earned by an affiliated licensee to a partnership, association, limited liability company, limited liability partnership, or corporation that is not licensed as a real estate broker on the condition that all of the following conditions are*

satisfied:

(1) At least one of the partners, members, officers, or shareholders of the unlicensed partnership, association, limited liability company, limited liability partnership, or corporation holds a valid and active license issued under this chapter.

(2) At least one of the partners, members, officers, or shareholders of the unlicensed partnership, association, limited liability company, limited liability partnership, or corporation is the affiliated licensee who earned the fee, commission, or other compensation.

(3) The unlicensed partnership, association, limited liability company, limited liability partnership, or corporation does not engage in any of the acts specified in division (A) of section 4735.01 of the Revised Code.

(4) The broker verifies that the affiliated licensee complies with divisions (C)(1) and (2) of this section and keeps a record of this verification for a period of three years after the date of verification.

(5) The broker keeps a record of all of the following information for each transaction, for a period of three years after the date of the transaction:

(a) The name of the affiliated licensee who earned the fee, commission, or other compensation;

(b) The amount of the fee, commission, or other compensation that was earned;

(c) The name of the unlicensed partnership, association, limited liability company, limited liability partnership, or corporation to which the broker paid the affiliated licensee's fee, commission, or other compensation.

The preceding very clearly shows that real estate agents in Ohio can have their commissions paid into the S Corps under state law; the problem is the bookkeep staff at many brokers or the brokers themselves simply do not know the law or just don't want to do it. There is no legal prohibition whatsoever, though, so we've had clients just show the broker the law to convince them.

Since having an S Corp can save a Real Estate Agent so much money, it would be helpful if this information were more widely known in the state's Real Estate Community.

You'll want to make sure that your commissions are paid to the S Corp, the checks are written to the S Corp, and the W9 and EIN you provide to the broker all accurately reflect the S Corp's information so the 1099 is made out correctly. If they still pay you under your Social Security Number and not the EIN, it ruins the whole point of the entire exercise.

You are still licensed as an individual Real Estate Agent, and you'll still be conducting business under your own name, advertising under your own name, have your sales license in your own name, etc.

The only thing that will change is you'll have a new bank account, and file as an S Corp to take advantage of the related tax savings. Your broker may ask for a copy of your corporate charter or LLC paperwork with the State, your CP 575 EIN notice from the IRS, or a copy of your operating agreement if you have one, and it's perfectly fine to get them a copy.

LOCAL TAXES FOR OHIO REAL ESTATE AGENTS

Ohio is a state blessed with 550 individual municipalities that tax its residents and everyone who does business in that municipality differently. Just about no two cities have the exact same tax rules and tax rates.

This is further complicated by the very nature of what most real estate agents do: Sell real estate in a variety of cities and townships.

Generally, you'd have to file a local tax return for each Ohio city in which you had a property sell. Your tax due to that municipality is based on an allocation portion of your net profit/(net loss) based on your profit percentage for all your closings.

Generally, since most real estate agents are self-employed, they are a sole proprietorship, and there is a 20-Day rule in Ohio for sole-proprietorships wherein they do not owe city tax if they work less than 20 days in that particular city during a tax year.

So if you had one house for sale in Akron, let's say, and your commission was $3,000, but you were only in Akron 5 days for that commission, you would not need to file a return for the city of Akron and would not owe them tax under Ohio law.

Many city tax departments are cracking down now on Real Estate Agents, particularly RITA communities (Ohio's Regional Income Tax Agency which collects taxes for many of Ohio's smaller cities) and are auditing Agents and asking for listings of all their closings and commissions for each sale.

The apportionment formula for city taxes is rather complex and we recommend having a tax accountant fully familiar with Ohio Tax for Real Estate professionals do it for you, especially if you have closings in multiple cities.

We've included a screen print from a city of Columbus return showing their allocation section:

City	Code		Column A Property	Column B Gross Receipts	Column C Wages	Column D Average %	Column E Allocated Net Profits
Columbus	01	a	$	$	$		$
		b	%	%	%	%	
Groveport	09	a	$	$	$		$
		b	%	%	%	%	
Obetz	10	a	$	$	$		$
		b	%	%	%	%	
Canal Winchester	11	a	$	$	$		$
		b	%	%	%	%	
Marble Cliff	13	a	$	$	$		$
		b	%	%	%	%	
Brice	14	a	$	$	$		$
		b	%	%	%	%	
Harrisburg	16	a	$	$	$		$
		b	%	%	%	%	
Everywhere Else		a	$	$	$		$
		b	%	%	%	%	

Agents who work more than 20 days in a city in which they have a sale must do a tax return for that city and file and pay any tax due accordingly.

We had a client for whom we had to file nineteen (19) different city returns, and he sold many houses in most of those 19 cities.

To say this is burdensome on real estate agents is an understatement! As with everything else, please consult your tax professional on city tax returns, they are every bit as complicated as Federal returns and the software-in-the-box really cannot keep up with City returns. You may need more help!

GET STARTED NOW!

Many readers probably already started planning out some steps they plan to take to save more money; and many of you have implemented some of the material from this system already. I say: Great!

We've tried to make it as simple-to-follow as possible, and we *are* in the full-time business of working with real estate agent clients. If you are a real estate professional who's reached the point where you don't have the time or inclination to spend six hours trying to do your own taxes, give us a call. (And most non-accountants spend more than six hours, with preparation, record-gathering, etc. – and still don't have the tax knowledge you now possess with this system!)

If you look at what you'd earn in commissions if you spend a solid six hours working hard to get a list or close a sale, you may find that what you pay a professional accountant will save you a lot of money just by freeing up some time and allowing you to do what you do best: making money selling real estate.

The biggest point I can emphasize is that if you're are going to skip around the manual and just read items that appeal to you, that you go through the Quick-Start Guide and go over those items first. That's where you'll save the most money.

Start saving money right now!

Made in the USA
Monee, IL
21 March 2021